TRAVELING WITH MATTHEW

Traveling with Matthew

How Does a Gospel Mean?

JAMES W. HULSEY

WIPF & STOCK · Eugene, Oregon

TRAVELING WITH MATTHEW
How Does a Gospel Mean?

Copyright © 2021 James W. Hulsey. All rights reserved. Except for brief quotations in critical publications or reviews, no part of this book may be reproduced in any manner without prior written permission from the publisher. Write: Permissions, Wipf and Stock Publishers, 199 W. 8th Ave., Suite 3, Eugene, OR 97401.

Wipf & Stock
An Imprint of Wipf and Stock Publishers
199 W. 8th Ave., Suite 3
Eugene, OR 97401

www.wipfandstock.com

PAPERBACK ISBN: 978-1-6667-0069-5
HARDCOVER ISBN: 978-1-6667-0070-1
EBOOK ISBN: 978-1-6667-0071-8

06/23/21

Unless otherwise noted, Scripture quotations are from the *New Revised Standard Version Bible*, copyright © 1989 National Council of the Churches of Christ in the United States of America. Used by permission. All rights reserved worldwide.

Scripture quotations marked NEB are taken from the *New English Bible*, copyright © Cambridge University Press and Oxford University Press 1961, 1970. All rights reserved.

To Joanna, whom I continue to receive as the gift she is; and to Emily and Robert, our children, whose lives continue to bless.

To the Mini Ecumenical Council, Eric, Phil, and Vic, in whose company I have known grace.

Contents

Acknowledgements | ix

PROLOGUE
Traveling with Matthew: *How* **Does a Gospel Mean?** | 1

CHAPTER ONE
Theme As Part of the Story | 5

CHAPTER TWO
Why Matthew? | 13

CHAPTER THREE
What is Our Landscape? | 20

CHAPTER FOUR
Keeping Step with Matthew | 28

CHAPTER FIVE
In Our Need | 40

CHAPTER SIX
Fragmentation and Reduction | 47

CHAPTER SEVEN
Jesus, the Message, and the People | 56

CHAPTER EIGHT
God's Grace and Demand and Our Confusion | 63

CHAPTER NINE
The Joy of the Kingdom | 72

CHAPTER TEN
The Swirl of Life Around Jesus | 77

CHAPTER ELEVEN
The Content and Vision of the Kingdom | 89

CHAPTER TWELVE
Jesus and the Torn Temple Curtain | 98

CHAPTER THIRTEEN
Belonging and Identity | 108

CHAPTER FOURTEEN
Wide and Deep | 117

CHAPTER FIFTEEN
Lost in Matthew, Chaos and Hope | 126

CHAPTER SIXTEEN
To Imagine a Language | 136

CHAPTER SEVENTEEN
Gathering Threads within a Theme | 145

CHAPTER EIGHTEEN
Back to the Beginning and with God to the Future | 155

EPILOGUE
On Going out the Door | 160

APPENDIX
Confessing Christ for Today | 165

Bibliography | 171

Acknowledgements

I AM INDEBTED TO the Rev. Dr. Victor L. Hunter, whose counsel and friendship has enriched this project. Also, I value the encouragement and support of Dr. Allan H. Cole Jr., who inspired me to persist.

I also gratefully acknowledge all that I have learned and loved with the West Islip Church of Christ, the Community Presbyterian Church of Malverne, the First Presbyterian Church of Smithtown and the Hudson Memorial Presbyterian Church.

PROLOGUE

Traveling with Matthew
How Does a Gospel Mean?

IN 2011, ON A Lilly Grant, I attended the Summer School of Theology in the historic English university town of Oxford. I had registered for a class on Matthew's Gospel because I had been nursing a hunch. It seemed to me that "God with Us" serves as bookends for Matthew. At the beginning, "'And they shall name him Emmanuel,' which means, 'God is with us'" (Matt 1:23). And at the end, "I am with you always, to the end of the age" (Matt 28:20).

Once, years before, I had read Robert Alter's *The Art of Biblical Narrative*, in which he observes that it is worth our while to pay attention to the beginning of a new narrative.[1] Biblical writers often alert us to character and themes through recurring words. For example, in the first three verses of Genesis 12, God speaks to Abram. The first person pronoun "I" is used or implied six times in the NRSV translation. In short space, this repetition on the divine side of the dialogue more than hints that God is the subject of the journey of faith to come.

Though Alter's study of biblical narrative refers to the Hebrew Bible, what if Matthew could be seen in the same light? He was certainly steeped in the old scriptures. So I tucked this thought away and took it to Oxford.

The class was taught by Dom Henry Wansbrough, an eminent scholar and delightful teacher. At break one morning, I had occasion to offer my hunch. Dom Henry's positive response let me know that I had stumbled onto something of value, like a pearl of great price. Since then other scholars have caught my attention with their focus on "God with Us."

---

1. Alter, *Biblical Narrative*, 74.

Let's begin by scratching this itch. Since Matthew is telling us the story of God with Us, what does the author want us to know? I invite us to read Matthew as a whole to see what the evangelist says about Jesus of Nazareth to actual people, followers of Jesus, later in the first century. In doing so, we may resist a reading that indulges in decontextualized generalities of the words of Jesus and his Gospel interpreter. By opening our minds and hearts to understand Jesus in his context as seen in Matthew, we can move to a later first century context and be better prepared to hear Matthew's message today. In short, this is a study of Matthew as a kind of journey across three landscapes: that of Jesus' day; that of fifty or so years later in Matthew's Jesus communities; and that of our own day, as we follow the trajectory of Matthew's Gospel to the present.

I take this journey as a retired preacher and pastor, exploring a hunch. For over forty years, I have put my hunches to congregations to draw them into quests for what the Spirit may be doing through Scripture with and among us. I invite you along.

Before we get right to it, we should keep in mind that the Gospels are interwoven with a kind of verbal artistry, poetic prose, we might call it. The American poet John Ciardi once entitled a book *How Does a Poem Mean?* In a recorded lecture from 1962 (now on YouTube), he says, in essence, that he is tired of the old classroom question, "What does this poem mean?"[2] The very form of a poem may be to delight or to hint, and to otherwise express in a "venture" of language what a person "experiences."

Borrowing from John Ciardi, How does Matthew tell us his story? I vary Ciardi's title from poetry to gospel, not to claim that gospel is poetry but that its meaning is as much in the *how* of it as in the *what*. God with Us is a way of being in flesh and history that we must encounter more than we can explain. Matthew has ventured a form of language to gather up how and why Jesus of Nazareth mattered to those first disciples.

We should not discount creativity in the Gospel writers as if to discard it to a trash bin of fiction, meaning untruth. Serious biblical scholars recognize the power of storytelling to accomplish the work of the message, not to mention to engage the imagination. That is my way of saying that the Gospels were not written as a kind of "Where's Waldo" for academic sleuths whether to prove or disprove certain theories but as texts on tiptoe to get us to see what they see.

I hasten to add that this does not mean we should dodge tough questions about the Bible. They abound, and we must grapple with them.

---

2. Ciardi, "How Does a Poem Mean?"

But the people who wrote the Gospels were themselves in the grip of something powerful and profound. Their efforts to express how God stepped into history have undergone the challenge of their subject. This includes the faculty of imagination. How does anyone glimpse the presence of God? "Just the facts, ma'am," may not get at the one who walked the hills in Galilee and welcomed the little ones at his feet, who later appeared to the women that first Easter morning and scared them to life. Imagination may be what God's Spirit stirs in us to travel the way that Jesus in Matthew calls us to go. At least, it may serve us to read this and other Scriptures with an openness to the intersection of God and life.

What Kind of Book Is This?

My dear friend, the Rev. Victor L. Hunter, once directed a retreat center that had a pub in its basement. He named it the Hope and Grapple. I like that because it is how we often attend to life. Whether on a bar stool or at an AA meeting, we hope and grapple. Or, we might reverse the order and say, "We grapple in hope."

One definition of grapple is "to engage in a close fight or struggle without weapons." Synonyms are wrestle, struggle, tussle. One usage is that "bad news is something it becomes necessary to grapple with (deal with)." I would say that Jacob's wrestling with the night messenger in Genesis 32 is a form of grappling with the holy.

In relation to Scripture, there are a variety of questions, dilemmas, murky sayings, shades of night that surface our own deep questions about God and life. Some of these can give way to the light of new information. Others are not penetrable by our minds alone, if anything is. And there are steps in between. So, we grapple.

But we grapple in hope that we are wrestling with God and God is wrestling with us. I have come to believe in life as well as in Bible study that whether we be in church, an AA meeting, or a pub, we do better to share our steps with one another. I offer this piece of writing in that spirit.

Throughout there will be sections I call Hope and Grapple. These will address hard questions or murky topics about the biblical text. And they will treat Matthew as a guiding light for the early 21st century.

Engaging with Matthew as I am, my intention is not to go a mile wide and an inch deep. A serious Bible student should have the baton of a particular text in hand before running with it. Upfront I must say that I am viewing Matthew as a whole literary unit. However the evangelist draws upon the Old Testament, the other Gospel writers, or unknown sources of

Jesus memory, he gathers them all into a coherent presentation of Jesus of Nazareth. Of the way this Gospel writer develops the story, I want to ask: What themes emerge and how does the narrative shape the gospel message? How do these speak to faith communities later in the first century? How may they speak to us today?

At the same time, I promise to share my own tussles with the topics and at the table of life. Over the years, I have learned that congregations are often listening for a preacher or a teacher not to give answers, but to indicate that faith can make our way in the dark, or, maybe even more likely, keep us going when conventional maps have not charted any course.

One last word about what you are reading. This is not a commentary. Though I have some facility with New Testament Greek and have read any number of scholarly works on Bible and theology, I do not pretend to be an authority on Scripture. This is not an exhaustive work, treating all of Matthew or lingering long with every knotty passage. This is more of an extended sermon with notes. For anyone who has got this far, it probably goes without saying that by sermon, I do not mean the kind of preachments that offer you and me the recipe for our lives. Rather, I mean the kind of sermon that invites us on a journey to follow the one who calls, saying, "Come, unto me" (Matt 11:28).

CHAPTER ONE

Theme as Part of the Story

MATTHEW BEGINS IN A unique way, as do each of the four Gospels. Why Matthew does so is not my immediate interest. Rather, I want us to identify how he does so.

One cannot get on with the first Gospel without slogging through the swamp of "begats." "The book of the heritage or lineage of Jesus Christ who is son of David and son of Abraham" (Matt 1:1) may be an awkward translation, but I like it better than the word "genealogy." "Genealogy" has the modern ring of someone looking back to find her or his identity, these days through DNA.

When I watch all the ancestry commercials on TV, I wonder what draws us to them. We know today that DNA studies show that human beings around the globe are more alike than we are different. I understand a modest curiosity about where we came from. But I am also leery of anything else that pits us against one another as different tribes.

Jesus was certainly Jewish, and we should understand him in that history and context, but he was not tribally so. There is something contra-Matthew if we stop with his Jewishness in 30 CE. Rather, Matthew is drawing an old story forward by using the names of its principal players: Abraham, David, and Mary. Along the way are the major developments: the kingdom of David, the deportation into Babylonian exile, and the birth of Jesus who is called Christ. More than a ponderous list of names, this caravan of people is moving with purpose. Significantly, the names of foreign women, Tamar and Ruth, Rahab, and the wife of Uriah, abide this genealogy and confirm Matthew's purpose to let the light of Israel shine for all people.

Now, quickly to the miraculous nature of Jesus' birth. Without dodging anything, I must say that too much ink has been spilt on it. Yes, there is a miracle here, but it is not a litmus test for sorting between conservatives and liberals. Bigger picture, Matthew's whole gospel message is miraculous because it is God's doing. Just as God was breathing through the old story with Israel, so God is giving life to something profoundly new. Is this not a story about his and our ultimate origins?

Joseph is understandably surprised by Mary's pregnancy. It takes the reassurance of the angel to keep him on track. But the message of the angel does not get lost in a discussion of whether or not Mary can be with child without having sex.

The angel is our first speaker, serving as a bridge to the past. "Look, the virgin shall conceive and bear a son, and they shall name him Emmanuel" (Matt 1: 23). Can "parthenos" be translated "young woman" or should it be translated "virgin"? That's not the translation that Matthew wants us to get right. Rather, his concern is about Emmanuel. If any Gentiles at the Seder don't understand the Hebrew, Matthew wants to make certain by adding, "which is to be translated, 'God is with us'" (Matt 1:23, mine).

Another candidate for a theme statement might be what the angel had said to Joseph in the dream a couple of verses earlier. "You are to name him Jesus, for he will save his people from their sins" (Matt 1:21). Jesus is itself a variation of Joshua, both meaning "savior."

No question, Jesus' role as savior from sins is paramount to understanding him. But I caution us not to pass by as if this is old hat. Note what the angel actually said, "He will save his people from their sins." Is there a different understanding of saving from sins when it applies to a whole people distinct from thinking of a people as a collection of individuals?

Back to the swamp of begats and the reference to "the deportation to Babylon." Isaiah, speaking the Word of God to the returning exiles, proclaims, "Speak tenderly to Jerusalem, and cry to her that she has served her term, that her penalty is paid" (Isa 40:2).

They had been told that the exile to Babylon was a punishment for their turning away from God. The release from exile was interpreted as forgiveness for what had sent them there. "She has received from the Lord's hand double for all her sins" (Isa 40:2). Enough is enough.

But in Jesus' day, Israel is in a kind of exile in its own land. They are occupied by their Roman overlords. The New Testament scholar N.T. Wright posits that it is not farfetched, but rather essential, for us to imagine that the people of Israel still saw themselves in exile.[1]

Did Matthew include the deportation simply as a convenient relief from the tedious reading of all those names? Luke does not include it in his

---

1. Wright, *New Testament*, 150.

comparable list of names (Luke 3:23–37). Or, was there something to this pulsation of events in Jesus' line? The people as a whole were still in need of a Savior.

As we move on, we need to keep the people as a whole and salvation from sins together. Even as we reach back to bring the story forward to our day, the church should acknowledge our sins as a whole. For one thing, the corporate or public nature of confession of sins keeps us connected to one another and to the larger play of events in our societies.

Life is complicated in the way that various conflicts are acted out in families and neighborhoods, whether locally or among nations. Within them, individuals become enmeshed and lose any righteousness to plead. I have heard it variously attributed, but nonetheless, it rings clear that "in almost any conflict, truth is the first casualty." We must always keep this larger context of sin in view.

Attending the whole landscape of wrongdoing cautions us against collapsing forgiveness of sins into our individual, private worlds. No question, sins are committed by individuals who should be responsible for them. It is also true that there are psychological dynamics that can haunt us like demons. But our ambitions, our desires, our fears, our idolatries have public faces as well. Whether it be the confessional or the corporate confession of sin, what gets confessed is more often than not sin in relation to. Sin has a story, and often it is about a tangled web in which we as individuals have gotten caught.

To enter the world of the Bible, and, in our case, Matthew, we must keep before us that Jesus always comes to save a people from their sins. Jesus enters that tangled web. Individuals are sinners within it, but sin is most often about what has gone wrong in relationships of varying kinds. Sometimes when we cannot sort out what we have done wrong and assessing blame gets us nowhere, we still know that we are in need of a savior.

Even so, I underscore that *God is with us*. I am making the case that this is Matthew's overall theme. More than the miraculous birth of Jesus, "God is with us" accents the truth that God has stepped into history. "Incarnation" is the traditional theological word to indicate God in the flesh or the divine word made flesh.

By the time that the theology of the incarnation got worked out in the great creeds, they understood Matthew and other New Testament writers to have articulated this truth. But we don't need to create a chasm between the ancient church creeds and the biblical writers to realize that Matthew is saying something more about God with Us than Jesus taking on flesh at one moment in history.

I began with a hunch about God with Us serving as bookends for Matthew. In the last words of the Gospel, Jesus says, "I am with you always, to the end of the age" (Matt 28:20). New Testament scholar Richard Hays called my attention to the third variation on this theme in Matthew: the familiar verse in 18:20, "where two or three are gathered in my name, I am there among them." Hays also enriches the theme as an echo of Genesis 28 which we'll consider later.

I believe Hays' reading is right, but I applaud more his imaginative work on the whole of Matthew.[2] We modern readers, including even preachers and scholars, shouldn't be quite so flat-footed in pursuing paths where the Gospels lead us. There is a captivity to literalism in our reading of Scripture from which we need release. We jail truth in our linguistic prisons, so that we cannot perceive with what breadth and depth biblical language attends to God.

I am old enough to remember a TV show called *Dragnet*. Whenever the no-nonsense detectives would go to someone's home to question an eyewitness, their standard line was, "Just the facts, ma'am." But a "just the facts, ma'am" or "mister" approach to Scripture won't do. By and large, the texts of the Bible are straddling the reality of God and the world as they knew it. Since by definition, God transcends the facts as we know them in the day-to-day world, to reduce language about God in narrative and poetry to the way we might describe the workings of a car engine, is to exclude God from the outset. More on this as we continue. How does Matthew bring the old story of Israel forward?

A Story Within the Story

Related to the theme, the first quote in Matthew from the Old Testament is, "Look, the virgin shall conceive and bear a son, and they shall name him 'Emmanuel,' which means, 'God is with us.'" (Matt 1:23). This is the first of nine quotes from the Old Testament that occur in the first four chapters, including the back and forth between Jesus and the tempter in chapter 4.

Already we have noted the connecting lineage with which Matthew begins. In addition, the spate of Old Testament references emphasizes this Gospel's concern to relate to and forward the old story of God with Israel.

The quote from Hosea, "Out of Egypt have I have called my son" (Matt 2:15; Hos 11:1), starts a journey. Matthew places Jesus with Mary and Joseph in Egypt and identifies him with Israel as a son coming out of that land of slavery. In the next chapter, Jesus journeys to the Jordan to be baptized

---

2. Hays, *Reading Backwards*, 38.

by John the Baptist. His baptism in the Jordan bears kinship to Israel whom God brought through both the Red or Reed Sea and the Jordan into the promised land.

But first Israel wandered in the Wilderness of Sinai for 40 years. It is no coincidence that Matthew has Jesus tempted in the Judaean Wilderness after he has not eaten for forty days and nights. Anyone familiar with Israel's story would know that the wilderness was also a place of temptation and testing for them.

And then Matthew has Jesus go up on the mountain for the Sermon on the Mount. Luke, by contrast, situates this sermon on a level place. None other than Moses went up on Horeb or Sinai to meet God and to receive the Law in the wilderness. Jesus' voice in Matthew resonates with authority that the people acknowledge is different than their scribes (Matt 7:29).

In Matthew, there are certainly other glances back at Israel's story with God, but the evangelist gets us going by taking us to and leading us through Israel's story in its "root experience."[3] Not only that, Matthew places Jesus within Israel's story. He walks with Israel, so to speak.

And just as the names at the beginning are more than a plaque of church pastors in the narthex, so the underlying story interwoven with the story of God with Us moves us forward. How it means is what it means. The way Matthew develops this Gospel, not only what he says, flirts with the reader's imagination. To my mind, Jesus is part and parcel of the continuing story of God with Israel. Jesus does not leave Israel behind. Jesus embodies God with Israel. Jesus brings the story to fulfillment.

Pausing for a deep breath, let's say again, Jesus does not leave Israel behind. We read that in how Matthew aligns his hero with the old story. We read it when Jesus says, "do not think that I have come to abolish the law or the prophets; I have not come to abolish but to fulfill" (Matt 5:17).

I must say here that our modern interfaith dialogue between Christians and Jews comes to mind on almost every page of Matthew. And well it should, because Christians particularly need to understand Jesus in Matthew as he relates to the Judaism of his day; or, perhaps better to say, the Judaisms of his day. Though I, as a Christian, come down on the side of Jesus as the embodiment of God's story with Israel, I must constantly ask myself what that means for my understanding of Matthew.

Truth to tell, I have said in sermons that the question for those who wrote the New Testament was not, "Will the Jews be saved?" Like the Apostle Paul, they could not see how God could revoke Israel's election and the promises. Rather, the message of the New Testament is that the Gentiles

---

3. Fackenheim, *God's Presence*, 8–14.

will be saved because God's work continues through the person and work of Jesus of Nazareth. And like Paul, who said, "God was in Christ" (2 Cor 5:19), Matthew saw in the person of Jesus the Christ, God with Us.

How can what God has done with and through Israel be reconciled with what God has done with and through Israel and Jesus Christ? Does this not leave us on the horns of a dilemma? Let us be careful about trying to resolve the unresolvable. I follow the great apostle who affirmed God's revelation to Israel and in Jesus Christ, both horns, and yet he looked to the horizon of God's mercy for all, concluding in doxology. Similarly, I confess Christ, not by presuming to understand how God will sort us all out, but by praising God from whom all blessings flow. For traveling with Matthew, it is best to say, Jesus does not leave Israel behind.

And yet, Matthew, more than the other gospels, places Jesus in the story of Israel in a way that moves the story forward. It is the way of a story that both undergirds and guides that captures my attention for today's church. Are we too close to it to notice how it means? Are we too entangled with the web of our society to notice that so many have lost touch with any story that undergirds and guides, gives us deep meaning and authentic purpose? I hope to whet our appetites for an exploration along those lines.

HOPE AND GRAPPLE

Now, for a grapple with Matthew itself. What kind of writing is it? I have overheard comments like, "It's the Word of God, and it says what it means and means what it says." And this from an actual bumper sticker, "God said it. I believe it and that settles it."

Were I mingling at a party when I heard such comments, I would probably take my drink and find someone else to talk with. Why? Because statements like that are actually conversation stoppers, not responses to questions.

Rather, a question is like a journey. We need a sense of how far we want to go with it before we set out. To drive down to the corner market for a carton of milk, I only need to grab the keys and hop in the car. But if I want to travel to Scotland, assuming I don't already live there, I must be prepared to dig a little deeper, asking things like, "What's the weather there this time of year?" and so on. How far do we want this grapple with Matthew to take us?

Also, a question is like a journey, not only pondering how far we want to go with it, but considering where we have started from in relation to where we want to go. When I led new member classes in a Presbyterian congregation, it was important for me to know what background the participants had.

Is this someone with little to no Christian upbringing whose knowledge is from what he has gleaned through attending worship here for six months? Or, is this someone who has extensive experience in the Christian faith from a Roman Catholic or Methodist church? Perhaps a certain woman may have served as an elder in two or more Presbyterian congregations. Given where the conversation needs to start with each person, I must adjust what I say.

Assuming we don't want to stop the conversation with slogan-like statements, what questions about Matthew do we bring to the table? Is Matthew, as a portion of Scripture, also the Word of God? Is Matthew inspired by the Holy Spirit? I would answer "yes" to both of those questions, but I must say that understanding the Bible to be the Word of God and inspired means to me different things than what I believed as a teenager.

Let's consider two confessional pieces of writing about the Bible, one from the Roman Catholic Church, the other from the Presbyterian Church USA. I preface these quotes by saying that I see no essential difference between them. First from Vatican II:

> Those who search out the intention of the sacred writers must, among other things, have regard for 'literary forms.' For truth is proposed and expressed in a variety of ways, depending on whether a text is history of one kind or another, or whether its form is that of prophecy, poetry, or some other type of speech . . . For the correct understanding of what the sacred author wanted to assert, due attention must be paid to the customary and characteristic styles of perceiving, speaking and narrating which prevailed at the time of the sacred writing.[4]

From "The Confession of 1967":

> The Bible is to be interpreted in the light of its witness to God's work of reconciliation in Christ. The Scriptures, given under the guidance of the Holy Spirit, are nevertheless, the words of (human beings), conditioned by the language, thought forms, and literary fashion of the places and times at which they were written. They reflect views of the life, history, and the cosmos which were then current. The church, therefore, has an obligation to approach the Scriptures with literary and historical understanding.[5]

Another way of phrasing the assumption that guides both these understandings is that the Sacred Scriptures are both the work of God and the work

---

4. Abbott, *Documents of Vatican II*, 120.
5. *Book of Confessions*, "Confession of 1967," Section C.2, 9.29.

of human beings. The Bible is the accomplishment of God's will in this written form, but through authors with all the limitations of human beings. The reality of God's Word transcends the Bible itself but that theological principle does not diminish the truth that the Bible is God's Word in written form. Though derived from the revelation of God to which Scripture attests throughout, the Bible is also a very human book in that sense of warts and all.

Guided by the church's teaching and scholarly work, I have come to believe that the Bible is not a uniform book with only one angle of vision. Rather, its multiple authors/editors over many centuries have provided different points of view. Sometimes they find themselves in tension with one another such as that between the writings that reflect Israel's tribal days which rub against certain views of the Davidic monarchy. In the New Testament, Jesus says in Matthew, "Do not think that I have come to abolish the law or the prophets; I have not come to abolish but to fulfill" (Matt 5:17). Compare that with what the Apostle Paul wrote in Romans, "Christ is the end of the law so that there may be righteousness for everyone who believes" (Rom 10:4).

These reflect both tensions and conflicts. I resist the word "contradictions," because it suggests a kind of either/or reading. Either/or can neglect nuance, context, and history. As a preacher/pastor, I am quite aware that a word for a grieving family may not be at all appropriate for a slanderous division in the congregation.

In this first Hope and Grapple, I am suggesting that we keep questions about Matthew open. Just about anything is fair game as long as it is a legitimate question and not a conversation stopper. How much actual remembrance of what Jesus said and did does Matthew represent? How much is his creative/theological interpretation?

Recognizing that these are good questions to which there are some significant responses is important for us. Admitting that we cannot know the answers to some good questions is also important on this journey.

There is a phrase in my Presbyterian tradition that expresses views we share with other traditions, "Obedient to the Word of God and guided by the Holy Spirit." The Bible is flat as the paper or screen on which we read it unless we seek the Divine Word that inspires it and pray for the Spirit's power that illuminates our minds and hearts. This understanding has saved me from what I believe is a life-strangling view of biblical texts that doesn't allow them either to speak for themselves or for God to speak through them.

CHAPTER TWO

Why Matthew?

A KNOWLEDGEABLE FRIEND ASKED me about this project, "Why Matthew?" It is a good question that I have begun to answer, but there's more which I want to cover in this chapter.

Basically I see across Matthew's landscape contours that resemble our modern situation. It has to do with bringing an old story forward, centering it around Jesus Christ, and offering listeners/readers a way forward in a strange new world.

I have already attempted to show how Matthew moves with the story of Israel to Jesus of Nazareth. When Jesus goes up on the mountain for the Sermon on the Mount, he is a kind of Moses but different. Why does Matthew relate Jesus to Moses, and why might that speak to his audience?

In his article on Matthew in *Reading Backwards*, Richard Hays compares one of the God-with-Us texts, Matthew 28, to Jacob's dream in Genesis 28.[1] On the threshold of the great mission of the church, Jesus says to the disciples, "I am with you always, to the end of the age" (Matt 28: 20)

In similar language, God, in Jacob's dream, says to him, "Know that I am with you and will keep you wherever you go" (Gen 28:15). Hays points out that the phrase, "I am with you" is nearly the same if we compare Jesus' Greek in Matthew 28 with the Greek translation of the Old Testament in the Septuagint[2] (the Greek translation of the Hebrew Bible; for Christians, the Old Testament). The only difference is that "you" is singular in Genesis but plural in Matthew.

---

1. Hays, *Reading Backwards*, 49.
2. Rahlfs and Hanhart, *Septuaginta*.

Given that Jacob's name change in Genesis 32 becomes the namesake of the people, I suggest there are more than a few Greek words and the name "Israel" that Matthew may be reaching back to bring forward. The dream/vision that Jacob has is a revelatory moment in the story, not only for him, but for Israel as a whole. It is no accident but the storyteller's art that the ladder connects God's presence with the people.

Having tricked his old, blind father Isaac to give him the paternal blessing that rightfully belonged to his elder brother Esau, Jacob is on the run. What will follow Jacob for the next twenty years is Esau's threat to kill him. As Jacob pillows his head on a stone that night, he is in a strange land, cut off from his past and uncertain about his future. "I am with you" greets him powerfully.

When Jacob arises, he says, "Surely God is in this place." I can't read this passage without hearing Bill Van Rosenberg's bass voice, just a bit shaky from age, yet nonetheless confident. He began the anthem with his a cappela solo, resonating richly in the sanctuary: "Surely God is in this place."

A bit shaky but nonetheless confident may describe Jacob in Genesis, and Bill van Rosenberg as a voice for the church today. How many people can resonate with that? Jacob was cut off from his past, in a strange land and uncertain about his future. Did Matthew have Genesis in mind as he wrote? Could he expect that his audience would think of the Jacob story? Obviously we cannot answer these questions for sure, but what we know is that Matthew is on the same page with the story of Israel and intends to bring it forward.

Imagine for a moment how Matthew's recipients were situated in the world. Perhaps needless to say, Jesus, the first disciples, and those early members of the first century church were Jewish. Not to acknowledge that fact raises a serious question about prejudice of an anti-Semitic kind. Early Christian conflicts about belief in Jesus as the Messiah may sound anti-Semitic to the modern ear, but we must remind ourselves that these were matters, in the early days, discussed among Jews. It is not even clear how many years after Jesus' death and resurrection it took for the Christians to become more than a sect of Judaism.

The harshness of Jesus' words in Matthew about the scribes and Pharisees are no harsher than the prophet Jeremiah's words against his own people. No one less than Elie Wiesel once wrote, "If anyone were to repeat today what he [Jeremiah] said about Israel, we would immediately call him an anti-Semite."[3] Wiesel said Jeremiah "assumed the role of a prosecutor" speaking for God against the people. Just as Jeremiah was inwardly torn

---

3. Wiesel, *Five Biblical Portraits*, 115.

apart by this assignment, Jesus weeps over his mission to Jerusalem (Matt 23:37; Luke 13:34).

This is not at all to deny anti-Semitism in Christian circles for the past 2,000 years. But when reading the New Testament, we must recognize that virtually all of the conflicts around things Jewish were in-house discussions. The Apostle Paul even wailed that he would willingly be anathema to Christ for the sake of his people (Rom. 9:3). So, by in-house, I mean among Jews, not necessarily over coffee and tea.

But with reference to words that are heard differently from time to time, more than once I have changed the readings of the passion narrative on Good Friday from the Gospel of John to Matthew because the recurrent reference to "the Jews" can sound anti-Semitic. And there is a long tradition of Christians using the Gospels to justify anti-Semitic prejudice. To pause to draw these distinctions is worthwhile both to read the New Testament more accurately and to acknowledge and address prejudice in modern congregations and the larger society.

As to the situation of Jewish Christians in the first century, Matthew wants them to know Emmanuel, that God is still with them. On the mountain, Jesus says, "Do not think that I have come to abolish the law or the prophets; I have come not to abolish but to fulfill" (Matt 5:17).

Too often any discussion of the Law of Moses (the Torah) in Christian circles takes on a Pauline flavor. To emphasize the importance of the Law in any way sounds like works righteousness to some ears. Jesus in Matthew and Jesus in Paul are pitted against each other. It is my view in these pages that though there are tensions between views of Christ and the Law between Matthew and Paul, they are looking at each from somewhat different perspectives, and we need both.

What was the importance of the Law of Moses for the Jewish people from Moses' to Jesus' day? The New Testament scholar Gerd Theissen says it well. "The Torah gave Judaism its identity, defined its privileged and perilous position among the nations and gave it its self-awareness."[4] I must take a moment with this trenchant observation.

Israel and Jews have often lived in hostile environments. The most immediate crisis before Jesus was the Maccabean revolt. It was precipitated when, in 165 BCE, Antiochus Epiphanes, ruler of Syria, had a pig slaughtered on the temple altar and placed a statue of Jupiter in that holy space. This sacrilege led to the overthrow of Syrian domination and political independence for the Jews for about 100 years.

---

4. Theissen, *Early Palestinian Christianity*, 77.

Against such hostility, Jewish moral and ceremonial laws kept the community intact. What outsiders might regard as quaint customs, Jews view as essential observances. Through devotion to God to keep the people holy as God is holy, Jewish religious practices are markers of identity in strong, not superficial, ways. The boundaries such markers keep relate directly to the God who keeps Israel. As Theissen notes, "the Torah gave Judaism its identity . . . and its self-awareness."[5]

Hopefully this makes more sense of Theissen's next remark. "Discussion of the true Torah and interpretation points to a crisis of identity within Judaism."[6]

Within Jesus' day and forward to the days of the early church, there was a crisis of identity for Jews. Here I am focusing on those persons who later in the first century read or heard Matthew about the years 80 to 95 CE. I am following the traditional dates that many scholars give for Matthew's writing. We will consider such issues later, but for now, I ask, what were Jewish Christians coping with about that time?

With the fall of Jerusalem to the Roman army (70 CE) during a long and bitter war, Judaism reached the end of an era. Two of the great symbols of Israel, the holy city and the temple, were in ruins. Jews and Jewish Christians were set adrift. They were cut off from the great story, hallowed by the giving of the Law, and thus separated from their historic identity. From our perspective so many years later, it is hard to overstate this crisis of identity.

But though Jerusalem had fallen and the temple was smoldering in ruins, the Law of Moses itself could not be taken away from them. We should recall that the early Christians yet had no Scriptures but the Hebrew Bible. But with the influx of Gentiles, the first great question that challenged Christianity became, "To what extent should the Gentile converts abide by the tenets of the Torah?"

Should Gentile men be circumcised? (The practice of female circumcision is nowhere mentioned in the Bible.) Should Jews and Gentiles keep a kosher table? Who can come to the table, that is, who is ritually clean and who is not? These questions speak to the practice of the new faith centered in Jesus. Faith is never merely theoretical. It is always a way of life. Jewish Christians wondered about leaving behind that way of life that had kept their people for centuries.

Jesus in Matthew addresses a number of these issues. He refuses to leave the Torah behind. Incidentally, Paul doesn't either. He just goes at it differently. But Jesus in the Sermon on the Mount begins to reinterpret the

---

5. Theissen, *Early Palestinian Christianity*, 77.
6. Theissen, *Early Palestinian Christianity*, 77.

way of the Torah. God with Us, the theme of Matthew, centers the retelling of Israel's story in the person of Jesus and what he does. The old story of God with Israel is so interrelated with Matthew that we must take pains to consider the false dichotomy between the two great testaments that often inhabits the Christian mind. (See the Hope and Grapple toward the end of chapter 4.)

For those reeling from being set out to sea, Jesus calms the storm. The old story now takes a new turn. Jesus in Matthew addresses three questions. One, have we lost all connection to Judaism? Without moorings to our past, how do we move forward? Two, certain teachers are pressuring us and the Gentiles to follow every tenet of the Mosaic Law. How much of it should we still keep? And three, the law of Moses was our orientation, our north star in a frequently hostile world. What identity now keeps us afloat and on course through the storm?

Hope and Grapple

I have been using phrases such as "Jesus in Matthew" and "Matthew does this and that." It is time to come to grips with what should be rendered to Matthew and what to Jesus in the Gospel of Matthew. But try as I may, sorting these things out is next to impossible.

Not too many years ago, a consortium of scholars made headlines by voting with colored marbles: white equals Jesus said it; black, he didn't. There were a couple of more or less likely votes in between. To my mind, this and similar approaches lose sight of the forest by examining the bark on every tree.

Still, we must consider the question of authorship. Only in Matthew does Jesus see and call a tax collector by that name. Mark and Luke mention the call of a tax collector but Mark calls him Levi, the son of Alphaeus, and Luke, only Levi. Does this suggest Matthew has subtly signed his portrait of Jesus?

In what follows, I am in line with the scholar Raymond Brown and his exquisitely informative *Introduction to the New Testament*. Several reasons make sense to me that Matthew, the apostle, was not the author. Beginning with this fact, Matthew "reproduces about 80 percent of Mark."[7] If the author of Matthew the Gospel was Matthew the eyewitness apostle, why would he need to draw so much on Mark?

---

7. Brown, *Introduction*, 171.

Second, nowhere in the gospel does the apostle step on stage and say, "I wrote this." The attribution of authorship occurred years later toward the end of the second century.[8]

The early church historian Eusebius (260–340 CE) quotes Papias (early second century CE) to say that "Matthew arranged in order the sayings in the Hebrew language, and each one interpreted/translated as he was able."[9] While the English translation of the Papias quote is murky, the Greek original is no more clear. By which I mean, though the scholars, being scholars, know their Greek, they are not sure what Papias meant by certain Greek words such as "logoi," translated "sayings."

This statement by Brown tickles my fancy: "Many would dismiss entirely the Papias tradition," but rescuing him from nonsense, Brown observes, "the fact [is] that ancient traditions often have elements of truth in a garbled form."[10] In other words, the ancient writers may very well have been making sense, but exactly what sense is lost to us. This is a subtle plea for humility, and it serves us well in reading the Gospels themselves.

The fact is that there is very little history (though a little) outside the New Testament that sheds definitive light on chronology, identity, and meanings that are obscure within the biblical writings. Educated guesses are what historical scholarship is all about. They help us to acknowledge our own biases and to read history and Scripture in better light.

But sometimes theories may be compared to the process of laying pavement: all mixed up and then set in concrete. "Do we really know this, or are we building castles in the air?" is always a relevant question, and scholars help us to distinguish between what we can know with a greater or lesser degree of certainty.

What we know of Jesus and the first-century world of Palestine from the texts themselves and scholarly work around the edges is not inconsiderable, particularly if we do not dismiss the New Testament out of hand as having no bearing on history. Many questions abound and should, but to my mind, there is no warrant for total skepticism, and more reason for trusting the reliability of the texts than some folks allow. Faith still seeks understanding, but faith that the New Testament has got Jesus right is not unreasonable.

As a preacher, dealing with Matthew and the like, I assume that the writer is in touch with the words of Jesus, though they may have come to him in a variety of ways. I also assume that the writer in his efforts to speak

---

8. Brown, *Introduction*, 208.
9. Brown, *Introduction*, 158.
10. Brown, *Introduction*, 161.

to the church later in the first century has re-formed and reemphasized. Like any good preacher, he has taken the main point and run with it. This is not to fictionalize Jesus, but to apply Jesus to people who are struggling with events and hard questions after Jesus.

Paul in his list of the gifts of the Spirit refers to both apostles and prophets (1 Cor. 12:29). What was a first century prophet after Jesus but one who spoke in the power of the Holy Spirit? Jesus in John's gospel says, "The Advocate, the Holy Spirit whom the Father will send in my name, will teach you everything, and remind you of all that I have said to you" (John 14:26).

In Matthew, Mark, Luke, and John, do we have prophets who spoke in the name of Jesus to address communities of faith in the early church? Did these persons see themselves empowered by the Spirit to speak the Word of God? Did they interpret the Old Testament to refer to and craft their understanding of Jesus? Was this God's way of advancing the gospel?

The view implied here suggests that the work of inspiration has suffered an all-too-narrow definition. God's Spirit breathes more freely in and through Scripture. Through transmission of Jesus' own words and deeds, through creative expansion of nuggets of information, through sayings and stories shared in worship, through applying and developing what Jesus said for later use, the Spirit empowered their hearts and minds. Not the least of which, through the morning light of the resurrection, the Gospels came to be. God was with them.

CHAPTER THREE

What is Our Landscape?

Home is Elusive

ONCE ON A VISIT to see my mother, I borrowed her car to tour the old neighborhoods where I had grown up in that town. I turned down St. John Street where we lived when I started elementary school.

Across the street a favorite aunt and uncle lived when they adopted my cousin as a toddler. He is now in his mid-sixties. On St. John Street I learned to ride a bike and once flew over the handle bars, kissing the curb before we had been properly introduced. Not far from that accident, I sat in a bed of ants, but not long. I ran home screaming and stripping all the way to my front door.

My dad taught me to mow grass at the St. John house. It was a push mower with a rotation of blades, the old kind with no motor attached. There our house was not air conditioned, and I remember hot nights, trying to fall asleep, arguing with my parents about not being able to feel the breeze which they assured me they could feel from my bedroom doorway. But I was skeptical then and still am.

As I turned down St. John Street, I drove to the middle of the block, expecting to see the white clapboard bungalow with a small yet pillared front porch. But to my surprise, that home was nothing but a vacant lot.

I offer this story to illustrate an experience I share with vast numbers of people. A man from England in one congregation I served shared a quite similar story of going back home. But we need not find vacant lots where dwellings once stood to feel the loss of a once-familiar world.

This is a fact of human life, and I am gesturing to the reality of a fast paced existence wherein we don't have to travel away from home to experience a dislocation from home. We no longer live in Alpine valleys where the village of this century is much like it was in the last.

Change is the order of the day. In his book entitled *Tangled World*, the Christian ethicist Roger Shinn quotes James Reston, the New York Times Washington Bureau chief. "Change is the biggest story in the world today, and we are not covering it adequately."[1] Reston wrote that in 1963. How much more is it true today?

And if change is the order of the day and home is elusive, the contours of our landscape are not dissimilar from those that Matthew traveled. Like Jacob before him, he pillowed his head in a strange land, cut off from his past and uncertain about the future. Though this could be said about many people in history and the present, the particulars are what bring in line the Old Testament story, the New, and the neighborhoods of our dislocation today.

Since World War II

The great film by William Wyler, *The Best Years of Our Lives* (1946), depicts a generation returning home from WWII. Through the lens of three soldiers, Wyler shows the struggles of so many. In one scene, Al Stephenson, a returning army sargeant played by Fredric March, walks down a long hallway, followed by the camera, which takes us on his return journey to his apartment door.

Finding one's way again in society is not easy for these military men. Wyler well deserves his honors for treating their stories with painful honesty. Post-traumatic Stress Disorder was not yet a diagnosis, not until 1980, though shell shock began to be well-documented from 1915 and WWI. Scenarios of coping with the loss of limbs, seeking acceptance from loved ones, and reentering business only to find it callous towards the very people who fought for the nation distinguish the three situations of the characters in the film.

My interest in this classic film has to do with how dismissive society later became of the 1950s. No doubt, it is a far cry from *The Best Years* to the world of *Leave It to Beaver*, but the two are related in my mind. Unless we understand something of what life was like for the returning veterans and those who kept the fires burning at home, we cannot understand with what gusto the nation returned to a version of normalcy in the 1950s.

Building homes, having families, and going to church were, for many Americans, the top three rungs on a ladder that would return them

---

1. Shinn, *Tangled World*, 8.

to normal life. Their rebellious children did not see life the same way, but neither did they see the suffering that generation had to endure. My father spoke very little to me about the war. He made curious references to it which I still wonder about, but like many of his generation, he did not talk about it very much.

There have always been some who like to tell war stories with great bravado, and others who flee to the next room when such conversations break out. Minus the bravado, is it inevitable that we go on with life without adequately passing on deep experiences from generation to generation? Generational differences are like separate rooms of conversation. Though it may be easy now to criticize the 1950s and the story of the mostly white America I am holding in retrospect, we cannot ignore the sacrifice and suffering that went into the new foundations they had to lay.

In our fast-paced society, we not only forget, but we run from our history. As with WWII, the past for some is too hard to speak of while others of us shut our ears to stories not our own. Yet, the world requires a much wider spectrum of storytelling to enlighten all of us concerning our neighbors.

It is my conviction that Matthew offers a way of bringing a great story forward that both interprets and shapes life without ignoring wrongdoing and tragedy. It is a story that can deepen our particulars. When *Leave It To Beaver* became the face of the 1950s, too many assumed that the status quo had taken no journey to get there.

A 2002 film by Todd Haynes entitled *Far From Heaven* drew attention to the moral fissures of life in 1950s Connecticut. The title itself takes a shot at the world of *Leave It to Beaver, Father Knows Best, Ozzie and Harriet* portrayed on television, if not many actual situations in Connecticut and elsewhere. Without question, it was necessary to revisit that history, but it was not an era without nuance and texture.

Matthew not only challenges us to deepen our understanding of particular stories, it broadens all perspectives. Not long after WWII and the Korean War had ended, the Montgomery Bus Boycott of 1957 caught the nation's attention. Dr. King and others brought civil rights to the public conscience. In those same years, my mother worked in the basement of a county courthouse that had restrooms and water fountains marked, "For Coloreds Only / For Whites Only." The sign over the main street in my hometown was, "Home of the Blackest Land and the Whitest People." Though years later many people would not deny prejudice there, some still tried to defend the old sign which had to be removed in the mid-60s. Sometimes the signs of racism above us speak more loudly than our willingness to acknowledge them.

As a result, many of the churches across the nation were slow to action related to civil rights, the feminist movement, environmental awareness, and, later, gay and lesbian rights, membership, marriage, and ordination. With these and issues of economic justice, the churches struggled and began to lose the support of a new generation. What their parents and grandparents had undergone that led to a new establishment was lost to the children and was, perhaps suppressed by many of the WWII generation itself.

Conflicts in the churches arose between those who sided with the new waves of social justice reform and those still hovering over the blueprints for new sanctuaries and education buildings. Sociologists studied this divide extensively. Peter Berger's *The Noise of Solemn Assemblies*,[2] Gibson Winter's *The Suburban Captivity of the Churches*,[3] Jeffrey Hadden's *The Gathering Storm in the Churches*,[4] and Dean Hoge's *Division in the Protestant House*[5] each dealt in part with an establishment church that could not keep up with its times and so resisted its Scriptures.

But did those who left the church house for the streets leave behind the great story? I am certainly not advocating a return to the "good ole days," because they were not good for many people. There was and is good reason to attend to those on the margins of society, whether their ancestors were the victims of slavery or suffered the indignity of drafty tenements without adequate water supply and sewage disposal. Whether from Europe, Asia, Africa, or Latin America, many were oppressed by those already settled here.

All the same, this nation has offered opportunity for many. Our history is a tale of two attitudes. On the one hand, we have welcomed countless millions to these shores, showing hospitality and good will for which Americans are famous. We cannot overlook the fact that Americans have big hearts toward neighbors at home and abroad who have suffered famine, natural disasters, and the ravages of war.

On the other, we have allowed fear of the other or the stranger to cordon off neighborhoods, establishing reservations for Native Americans, black and white segregation, internment camps for Asian Americans, and, more recently, walls of hostility against those fleeing extreme oppression in their own countries. And at its worst, our economy has been propped up by keeping others down.

2. Berger, *Noise*.
3. Winter, *Suburban Captivity*.
4. Hadden, *Gathering Storm*.
5. Hoge, *Division*.

Reacting to some of our worst tendencies, those who left the church and those who viewed religion as irrelevant contributed to a secular drift. Some, no doubt, maintained their ties to traditional faith and allowed its deep story to inform them. But no one can argue with the demographic decline of the "mainline" or "mainstream" houses of faith, as they were called. They no longer occupy their once central place in American life.

In addition to the divide around issues of social justice, we must own the rich color of diversity in North America, black, brown, red, white, and yellow, though we are actually a variety of shades. Then came migrations of persons who brought Hinduism and Islam (other beliefs as well) from their native lands. As many left traditional houses of worship, an interest grew in Eastern and Middle Eastern religions. This "turning east," or to Islam, contributed to the new contours of the religious landscape that can no longer be described as the sociologist Will Herberg did in 1956's *Catholic-Protestant-Jew*.[6] Buffeted by such change, what has happened to the Judeo-Christian narrative that was once familiar to most people?

A seminary professor told the story of visiting a New York museum that featured an exhibit honoring the accomplishments of women. Various facsimiles of great women were arranged in twelve seats around a table with a central figure as its host. My former professor heard a woman behind her say to another, "I get the importance of the women they have displayed here, but what's with this table and how the women are placed around it?" "I think it has something to do with the Bible," said the other. "I'll tell you later."

What I am getting at is not only the often-bemoaned climate of biblical ignorance. It is rather a society that is losing one story as its narrative with no other great story to replace it. Showing cause and effect is not easy to document in this respect. Even so, from the point of view of religious leaders, we have seen the effects of social mobility from one section of the country to another, and people choosing not to affiliate with any community of faith in their new neighborhoods. We know the drift of students going away to college who used to come back for marriages and baptisms but do so less frequently. And with many interfaith marriages, parents sometimes choose by default not to raise their children in any religious tradition, assuming they will find their way on their own.

Diana Butler Bass speaks to my experience and outlook with her discussion of the years 2000–2010 which she calls "The Horrible Decade."[7] Confidence in religious institutions was still high in the 1990s, but with the religiously-inspired 9/11 attacks, the vast clergy sex abuse scandals, and the

---

6. Herberg, *Catholic-Protestant-Jew*.
7. Bass, *Christianity After Religion*, 76–83.

awful rantings against gay and lesbian persons, many who formerly had positive views of religion now wanted no part of it. Over a period of years, Will Herberg's religious mainstream declined in numbers and no longer grabbed the headlines.

The new religious right replaced the older, established houses of worship. Often television reporters referring to Christians and churches mean those on the right, without acknowledging the diversity of Christian opinion. I believe that Bass has rightly called our attention to a decade of discontent regarding religious trust. Opinion polls support her analysis, and we are still living with the consequences of those years and many of their unresolved issues.

The point of this historical excursion is not to play the sociologist. I have referenced a number of good ones, but am not one. But as preacher/pastor, I have studied the context of both the churches I serve and the society that contains them. I have reason to believe that a version of this same brief history can be told from both a Roman Catholic and Jewish perspective. Though I stand by this overall arch of years from WWII to the present, I am first to acknowledge that such sweeping comments are wrong in some respects. There are many exceptions such as any number of clergy who lost their jobs because they addressed racism in their communities.

No doubt, there are others who have lived and followed this history who would want to include important events that I have not, such as the whole epic and tragedy of the Vietnam War and the debacle of Watergate, with its wake of distrusting people in power. My focus is more narrowly confined to society's loosening hold on a larger religious narrative, informed by the Scriptures of Israel and the Church.

Also, this is no diatribe against other churches, religions, or those who affiliate with none. I have relatives and friends among them all, as most of us do. And often those of no specific faith outshine me and people of my faith family in their commitment to social justice and their basic honesty and kindness.

Nonetheless, if we lose touch with our great stories, lesser stories take their place. The narratives that lead to greed and tribalism are two that plague this diverse land and its vaunted opportunity for all. If we do not live by a story that can affirm our best while challenging our worst inclinations, we will live by a lowest common denominator of "us and them" and "whatever it takes." These represent the slogan of the tribe and the mantra of greed.

Unstoried, we lose our way home. And without any sense of home, we forget who we are. Traveling with Matthew, we are searching for a way to tell our story that is as wide and forward thinking as the Great Commission (Matt 28).

Hope and Grapple

More thoughts on how we travel with Matthew: I have already hoisted a flag of respect for the work of biblical scholars. At the same time, I must acknowledge respectfully the work of the preacher, pastor, and Christian educator, which is different. While the scholar spends tiring hours trying to understand a worldview from ancient texts and artifacts, preachers and others work with ancient biblical texts while inundated with questions and points of view from the world all around them and within.

Years ago, I observed a seminarian teaching an adult Bible class in church. This man went on to become an outstanding scholar whom I respect, but his response that day to certain questions by congregants was, "That is outside my area of expertise." For those bridging academic studies to church classrooms, "that is outside my area of expertise" is a luxury rendered penniless in the economy of the ordinary world.

The preacher, pastor, educator are more like any version of the theologian in making the move from what the Bible says to what it means for us today. In fact, often when people open the Scriptures, they bring with them certain poignant questions or life situations; reading the Bible through tears, we might say.

The New Testament theologian Rudolph Bultmann spoke of the "presuppositions" of the Bible reader.[8] He was referring to the different worldviews that modern audiences bring to the text. That is certainly true, but given the nature of the Bible as a sacred text for Jews and Christians, there is an expectation that we can find divine help there. And that too is part of the "presuppositions" which we bring.

Bultmann and other scholars have been criticized for reading the Bible through the lens of modern philosophical viewpoints. Other scholars have raised concerns about stereotyping Pharisees according to modern prejudices that may offer Matthew as prooftext. For these reasons, one of the Ten Commandments of current scholarship is, "Thou shalt not impose the views of the contemporary church or world onto the biblical text."

The question I am raising is this: can we so situate an ancient text of Scripture in its context and worldview such that the distance to contemporary life is just too great to traverse? We could become like the Irishman

---

8. Bultmann, *Existence and Faith*, 290–291.

who was once asked for directions to Cork: "Oh, you can't get there from here".

Though I differ with Bultmann in a number of respects, I still appreciate his efforts to interpret Scripture for a modern audience. If that work cannot be done with some authenticity, the church might as well stay home on Sunday. Not a few folks have made that choice.

So, there's a tension between those who want to locate Jesus and the Gospels in their first-century Jewish context and those who want to understand Jesus and the Gospels for our lives today. The tension is not between believers and unbelievers in this instance. That tension exists in all of us. Rather, the tension has to do with the nature of the work itself.

To understand an ancient biblical text in its own context is a worthy occupation. To understand an ancient biblical text for its continuing relevance today is also a worthy occupation. But the two are often leaning in different directions and paying attention to different congregations, so to speak. And a number of people, like many preachers, pastors, Christian educators, theologians, thoughtful seekers and, without a doubt, biblical scholars live in both worlds.

I must admit my bias. Though I see clearly how easy it is to impose our modern views on ancient passages of Scripture, I also believe that it is easy for scholars who see themselves only at the work of doing history or ideas not to pick up on clues within the Bible that allow resonance with persons and times far removed from those days. I believe that Matthew gives us such clues, loud and clear. I believe the story of God with Us is Matthew's way of addressing a message to Christians in the 80s and 90s of the first century that also speaks to the twenty-first century.

CHAPTER FOUR

Keeping Step with Matthew

THE FIRST FEW CHAPTERS of Matthew give us a unique slant on the story of Jesus of Nazareth. As I have already said, from the begats at the beginning to the Sermon on the Mountain, the old story of Israel is being drawn forward. And it is wrapped around the person and work of Jesus.

As Matthew continues to tell the story, he follows Mark's gospel considerably. Again, the scholar Raymond Brown says 80 percent of Mark appears in Matthew.[1] Though Matthew improves Mark's Greek and varies some phrases, the second Gospel is quite likely a primary source for the first.

In addition to Mark as literary guide, Matthew likely shares another source with Luke. This is evident because Matthew/Luke has a number of sayings and stories which do not appear in Mark, nor in John, for that matter. Much has been made of a common source that the first and third Gospels draw upon. It has even been named "Q" by scholars, which is simply the first letter of "Quelle," the German word for source. Scholars have mused about one day discovering Q and learning more about the community that produced it.

But there is yet to surface an ancient Q scroll, nor, like the Qumran community, remains of a people who followed Jesus as they were guided by it. It makes perfect sense that Matthew/Luke draws upon some material of which they are both aware. Was it one or more sources? We don't know. Was there a particular community that had a unique view of Jesus that differs from the four Gospels as a whole? I find that to be a stretch.

---

1. Brown, *Introduction*, 171.

What we do know is that Matthew, Mark, and Luke are called the "synoptic Gospels" because they tend to see Jesus alike, that is, they present the Savior's story in similar ways. Though John has a different format and theological flavor, I do not find a different Jesus there, but another angle of vision. My point here is that Matthew, like the other three Gospels, though different, follows a similar story line.

The synoptic Gospels structure their story around an explicit journey to Jerusalem. Though John does not use the image of the disciples following Jesus on this journey to the extent that the first three do, there is no question that Jesus is stepping into the most significant events of his life as John draws to a close. The last few chapters of each gospel slow to a crawl with more verses and detail in the telling of Jesus' last meal, arrest, trial, crucifixion, and resurrection. Clearly this is the destination and dramatic climax for all four of the evangelists.

Though there are numerous discourses and sayings that offer their particular accents along the way, the Gospels progress in a similar way. The world of scholarship abides by making distinctions, but one would have to be blind to this literature not to see where it wants to take us. The one who proclaimed the kingdom, healed the sick, cast out demons, told parables, envisioned the fall of Jerusalem and the destruction of the temple was on a prophet's journey to the city that had been hard on past prophets.

The particular ending shared by the four was summarized earlier in the first century by the Apostle Paul. He wrote, "First and foremost, I handed on to you the facts which had been imparted to me: that Christ died for our sins, in accordance with the Scriptures; that he was buried; that he was raised to life on the third day, according to the Scriptures; and that he appeared to Cephas, and thereafterwards to the Twelve" (1 Cor. 15:3–5, NEB). Death, burial, and resurrection represent the key elements of Christ's concluding existence on earth.

Though the four Gospels include much more prior to Jesus' death, they nonetheless narrate a story that reaches its dramatic purpose in those events. Were one to cut off the ending from the scrolls of each Gospel, we might think of Jesus as a wonderful teacher, a great healer, a hardnosed prophet, but would he have been remembered much beyond the first century?

In fact, would he have called disciples to follow on this journey to death and life and later bid them proclaim that message to all the world? In this regard, the pages of the Gospels hand us characters with whom we may identify, not in their first-century dress, but in their life situations and struggles to understand Jesus. Among them are fisherfolk, a Canaanite woman, a tax collector, and even a zealot. They frequently did not get what he was doing or saying. As his ending was awful, so was theirs, in a different way.

As a literary device, the call to follow and the hard way they went reaches out to us.

We hear from Matthew 11 these words which have touched so many at funerals and on other difficult occasions: "Come unto me, all you who are weary and carrying heavy burdens, and I will give you rest. Take my yoke upon you, and learn from me; for I am gentle and humble in heart, and you will find rest for your souls. For my yoke is easy and my burden is light" (Matt 11:28–30).

In summary, this story is not a mere biography of some person of particular interest. It is a proclamation of "gospel" or good news, calling disciples to follow Jesus on a hard journey through death to life. That is what I believe Matthew's message was for those Christians, struggling to find their way in the 80s or 90s of the first century. He was not creating a piece of fiction about a person who was barely remembered. Rather, he was gathering from the considerable memory of past disciples to forward the story for a new day.

In the same way, that story speaks to us in a way that gives our lives meaning and purpose. Those of us who find ourselves in worship services hear it often. Sometimes so often, I think, that we take it for granted. Others of us, who are probably not reading this, have lost touch with the story. I have a heart for them and desire that we as a church articulate and live our message with the power it has. To my mind this task is uniquely urgent due to the speed and variety of means we have to go nowhere in particular.

With so many narratives pressing their claims to get us through our days, I wonder to what end? Nora Watson in Studs Terkel's book *Working* says, "Jobs are not big enough for people."[2] Traveling with Matthew, I search for life that will increase our spirits until we know they are made for more than burying our gifts and hiding from the persons we were created to be (Matt 25:24–25).

How Do We Learn the Story and What Distracts Us?

As you may guess, I will be saying that we learn the story through the church. But that is, nonetheless, a hard-won observation because I, like many others, understand her flaws.

Once a deacon said to me, "I liked the church better before I got on a board." A widely-quoted aphorism, attributed to a late medieval manuscript, has it that "the church is like Noah's Ark. Were it not for the storm on the outside, you couldn't stand the stench on the inside." Witty as it is, the

---

2. Terkel, *Working*, 613.

medievalist was both accurate and too strong at the same time. But I get the stench of the church and how it affects us, to put our negative reactions in their most visceral form.

Those who lead do not always live up to our expectations. Some fall far from any imitation of goodness, not to mention godliness. The sexual abuse crisis is gut-wrenching for those who have been its victims and for those who have given their lives in service only to see what a mess of it their colleagues and spiritual guides have made.

During church meetings and in parking lots afterwards, there can be endless talk. Some over important matters, but also the color and pattern of the new chairs for the parish hall. A number of us struggle with the trivialization of church life through our arguments about the purchase of chairs, the color of paint, whether or not to remove the front pews in the sanctuary. I realize, like anyone, that the church has practical matters to attend to. We are called to serve Christ on earth. Yet, rather than a faith that moves mountains, we too often make mountains out of molehills.

Most of us have heard folk say things like, "When I go to church, I don't want to get in the middle of something like office politics or arguments at home." There is a legitimate expectation of some taller stature of Christian existence in the church. Yes, we are as human as any others in our limitations and imperfections. That has rightly been emphasized for a while now. But shouldn't our lived responses to God's grace shine some light in the world and not be totally eclipsed by the shadows of our sinfulness?

Then, of course, there are many contemporary versus more traditional tensions. We might call this the "J.S. Bach versus Amy Grant divide." To my mind the cultural and stylistic tensions often do not get at the more central question of what should happen in worship. That is, do we sense that anything is happening whatever the style? When we dedicate time and space to come before God, it should not be business as usual.

On the one hand, the church over 2,000 years and in many locations has made adaptations related to its cultural context which will continue, and should. On the other hand, worship like a laser should fix our attention on God. Of course, our likes and dislikes inevitably enter into our planning, but no one's ego tethered to sentimentality or cultural preference should distract us from the importance of lifting all hearts to God.

Also, the often criticized institutional forms of the church frustrate many people. Should a budget guide us, or the needs we feel called to address? Should we vote by majority rule or be gathered into a consensus? Do we need all this property because we are spending so much just to repair the old steeple? Why should such a percentage of our offerings go to staff when there are many gifted people here who could volunteer their expertise?

My son raised a pointed question, essentially this: "Doesn't an AA meeting get people to open up about their flaws and helplessness much more than any Bible study or small group in church?" Surveys say that people are looking for belonging and intimacy. But the church wants new blood to serve on boards and committees. How is it that this organization which is supposed to gather us in community and send us out with the gospel seems interested only in warm bodies? Wouldn't time taken in prayer to discuss our own woundedness make us more available for the wholeness of others?

This is enough of "the stench" to surface our reactions and concerns about the church. But I must add that the church has struggled from the beginning with many similar matters. None of our struggles are exclusively modern, only some of the particulars. Returning to Matthew, what may have plagued first century Christian communities?

As was mentioned in chapter 2, there likely were Jewish Christians who were pressuring the fledgling churches to abide by the tenets of Mosaic Law. I offer two examples from Matthew.

The first, Matthew shares with Mark (Matt 15:1–20; Mark 7:1–23): "Then the Pharisees and scribes came to Jesus from Jerusalem and said, 'Why do your disciples break the tradition of the elders? For they do not wash their hands before they eat . . .' Then Jesus called the crowd and said to them, 'Listen and understand: it is not what goes into the mouth that defiles a person, but it is what comes out of the mouth that defiles . . .' But Peter said, 'Explain this parable to us.' Then Jesus said, 'Are you also still without understanding? Do you not see that whatever goes into the mouth enters the stomach, and goes out into the sewer? But what comes out of the mouth proceeds from the heart, and this is what defiles. For out of the heart come evil intentions, murder, adultery, fornication, theft, false witness, slander. These are what defile a person, but to eat with unwashed hands does not defile'" (Matt 15:1–2; 10–11; 15–20).

Jesus, by reversing inner and outer purity, did not go against the Ten Commandments, but he did offend a host of teachings and practices set up to distinguish between clean and unclean persons. "Who can come to the table?" was the question behind the purity code. Some thought only pure Jews could recline there. Washing one's hands was not only for hygienic purposes, but more a gesture of ritual purification. For Jesus to focus on what comes from the heart to indicate what makes one clean or unclean changes the whole criteria of Jewish identity. Even a Gentile could be pure with reference to "murder, adultery, fornication, theft, false witness and slander."

As an illustration of issues that Matthew may have been addressing, we read in Galatians where Paul says, "When Cephas came to Antioch, I opposed him to his face, because he stood self-condemned; for until certain people came from James [that is, Jerusalem], he used to eat with the Gentiles. But after they came, he drew back and kept himself separate for fear of the circumcision faction" (Gal 2:11–12). What is behind this is the question, "Can we Jews who are pure by race and ritual purity sit at table with Gentiles who are not?" There were apparently some Jewish Christians who thought that Gentile men should be circumcised, that is, obey this aspect of Mosaic Law and Jewish identity.

Paul goes on to say, "We ourselves are Jews by birth, and not Gentile sinners; yet we know that a person is justified not by works of the law but through faith in Jesus Christ" (Gal 2:15–16a). Paul would not have differed with Jesus in Matthew about insisting that Gentile Christians obey the commandments that Jesus cites in Matthew 15. At issue are the distinguishing marks of Judaism, such as circumcision, purity of race, ritual cleansing, and the like.

The question for scholars of Matthew is, "Did Jesus himself alter these marks of Judaism during his lifetime, or did Matthew apply Jesus to a later situation where, like Paul, he was dealing with pressures and demands from Jewish Christians in the church?" My view is that Jesus in his lifetime began to open the kingdom to those beyond the strict codes of purity.

In Matthew 9, the Pharisees grumbled about Jesus and his disciples eating with tax collectors and sinners. To which Jesus responded, "Those who are well have no need of a physician, but those who are sick. Go and learn what this means, 'I desire mercy, not sacrifice' [Hosea 6: 6]. For I have come to call not the righteous but sinners" (Matt 9:10–13).

Many scholars of varying viewpoints agree that Jesus' table community in the gospels was typical of him. He was open to more than the purest of Israelites according to the codes that restricted their identity. So I have no trouble viewing Jesus as introducing a new criteria of humanity during his ministry and Matthew applying it later in sharp opposition to persons who wanted to restrict all Christians to the narrow teachings that Jesus himself had opposed.

But back to those aspects of church life that offend people today, Matthew certainly had his tussles with those who wanted to be more righteous than Jesus, so to speak. In chapter 23, Jesus goes on a Jeremiad excoriating the scribes and the Pharisees. He is in full prophetic denunciation mode, and, as Eli Wiesel said about Jeremiah, "did we not know that he was a Jew, we might think him an anti-Semite."[3]

"The scribes and Pharisees sit on Moses' seat; therefore, do whatever they teach you and follow it; but do not do as they do, for they do not

---

3. Wiesel, *Five Biblical Portraits*, 115.

practice what they teach. They tie up heavy burdens, hard to bear, and lay them on the shoulders of others; but they themselves are unwilling to lift a finger to move them" (Matt 23:2–4).

Did Jesus say this, did Matthew, or does this reflect again Matthew taking Jesus and applying his teaching later on in the life of the church? I do not know for sure, though I am inclined towards the "some of both" school. What I do know is that Jesus hits the nail on the head of certain religious persons who set themselves above others, tighten the demands of God around their necks, and refuse to do anything but watch them swing at the end of a legalistic noose. "Woe to you, scribes and Pharisees, hypocrites! For you tithe mint, dill, and cummin, and have neglected the weightier matters of the law: justice and mercy and faith. It is these you ought to have practiced without neglecting the others. You blind guides! You strain out a gnat but swallow a camel" (Matt 23:23–24).

Yes, Jesus does say, "without neglecting the others." We all are busy with "the others," those ordinary matters of setting up communion, arranging flowers, preparing services, removing coffee cups from the balcony, rehearsing with choirs when work looms next day, and staying up late on a Saturday to go over the church school lesson. It is when we resent those who seem to glide through church without accepting any of these responsibilities that our ecclesiastical fatigue can develop a sharp tongue. "Justice, mercy, and faith" are still our reminders of deep breathing when we want to scratch the itch of dumping on others.

Exhausted by my own righteous indignation, I have found that spiritual practices can reset and recenter our perspective. Walking the labyrinth with youth in confirmation class, I have left arrogance and resentment behind as I moved to the center. Like Moses at the burning bush, I need to step from my protective leather to walk unshod before God and to feel the holy ground that upholds us.

As hard as it may sometimes seem, Jesus is with us "where two or three are gathered in my name" (Matt 18:20), and we feel most annoyed with them. The story that claims and defines can reemerge in our deepest need as we turn the pages of its life and ours and find ourselves unstuck and moving on through another season. How does this happen?

Hope and Grapple

Before going on to consider how our deep needs serve as entre to Jesus, we must take time to consider how the Hebrew Bible or the Old Testament is similarly our entre to understanding Jesus in Matthew. Let's remember:

"The steadfast love of the Lord never ceases, his mercies never come to an end; they are new every morning; great is your faithfulness. 'The Lord is my portion,' says my soul, 'therefore, I will hope in him.'" (Lamentations 3: 22–24) This is one of the greatest affirmations of God's love and care in all of Scripture. Ironically it occurs in the middle of a doleful lament about Israel's captivity to Babylon: "My eyes flow with rivers of tears because of the destruction of my people" (Lam 3: 48).

And yet, Christians persist in saying that the Old Testament pictures a god of wrath, while the New Testament pictures a god of love. Also that the Old Testament is a burden of legalism while the New Testament is a gospel of freedom. Such viewpoints are distorted generalizations which suffer from limited focus on some passages to the exclusion of others.

In addition to the wonderful affirmation from Lamentations (which has inspired Christian faith and hymnody), the Old Testament is rich with litany of God's love. Psalm 136, called the Great Hallel, is recited in its entirety on many Sabbaths and other festive occasions. Rehearsing in twenty-six verses the acts of God for which thanks should be given, each verse contains the refrain, "for God's steadfast love endures forever."

One need only note that Jesus took the two great commandments (love God and love your neighbor) from Deuteronomy 6:5 and Leviticus 19 18. In Matthew, Jesus says, "On these two commandments hang all the law and the prophets" (Matt 22:40). The Apostle Paul follows Jesus in summarizing obedience to God this way: "Owe no one anything, except to love one another; for the one who loves another has fulfilled the law" (Romans 13:8).

In a non-legalistic view of Israel's election, Deuteronomy bases the call of the people on God's love. "It was not because you were more numerous than any other people that the Lord set his heart on you and chose you— for you were fewest of all peoples. It was because the Lord loved you and kept the oath which he swore to your ancestors, that the Lord has brought you out with a mighty hand, and redeemed you from the house of slavery" (Deut. 7:7–8).

When the harpies of my mind are digging their claws into me, I have turned over and over to this marvelous verse from the psalmist: "As a father has compassion for his children, so the Lord has compassion for those who fear him. For he knows how we were made; he remembers that we are dust" (Ps 103:13–14).

And yet, from the beginning of Christian history, there were those who wanted to distinguish between the cruel god of the Old Testament and the god of love of the New. I am not denying that certain passages in Scripture can strike us as cruel, such as God striking Uzzah dead because he merely reached out his hand to steady the Ark (2 Samuel 6:6–7), or Jesus in Matthew calling the Canaanite woman "a dog" (Matt 15:26).

But when Marcion chose to develop a canon of Scripture, perhaps the first to do so, he eliminated the whole of the Old Testament from it, and most of the gospels, except for an edited version of Luke. He included nearly all of Paul's corpus, but left out other portions of the New Testament. The relevant question is why?

He seems to have been possessed by the view that God, by creating the world, sullied the divine nature with evil matter. In other words, any deity that mucks around with history too much cannot remain pure love. It makes sense that when the church labeled Marcion a heretic for aversion to holding creation and love together (he was formally excommunicated in 144 CE) most of his followers took up with the Manichees by the end of the 200s CE.

Saint Augustine left the Manichees after a nine-year sojourn with them because of their radical dualism, meaning that they divided reality into equal camps of good and evil. Christians have always had a healthy regard for evil, but believe that God has given the sign of its ultimate defeat in the death and resurrection of Jesus Christ.

Marcion and his followers were consistent in expunging their spirituality of material nastiness by denying that Jesus had actually died and risen bodily. Again God would not be so tainted with the muck of actual life. (Though the story of Marcion may be read in the likes of Henry Chadwick or Jaroslav Pelikan, I have most recently been refreshed by *The Oxford Dictionary of the Christian Church*.[4])

What a brief study of Marcion can demonstrate is the risk to faith of separating the Old and New Testaments. Involved is the separation of creation and God's love, which also entails the elimination from history of any view of God that smacks of human emotions.

Which brings me to how we read Scripture generally. As I discussed in chapter 1's Hope and Grapple, Roman Catholic and Presbyterian Church USA views of Scripture include the cultural views and attitudes of the writers at a certain period of history. Both views recognize the literature of Scripture to represent an understanding of reality at a given time. This does not mean for either that those views do not develop, even within Scripture.

To be as clear as I can, I grew up with a view that the Bible is a book of facts about God, the Church, and how we should behave to gain God's approval. In other words, it is a kind of divinely-inspired operations manual for the church. We were so focused on getting back to the blueprint of the

---

4. Cross and Livingstone, *Oxford Dictionary*, 870–871.

church in the first century that we took our eyes off God as the one to whom the Bible directs our attention.

Starting from a different assumption, which I do now, the Bible orients us as a testimony to God through God's story with Israel and Jesus Christ. With this different orientation, we develop another lens for reading. Basically we are no longer checking items off a list to get a logically tight view of God, nor satisfying requirements of our admission to God's kingdom and life everlasting.

Rather, we are accepting the great invitation to play a part in God's story. Though all the Bible is not set forth in narrative or story form, it is held together by the story of God with Israel and in Jesus Christ. As Bible readers and followers of Christ, we do not begin the journey of faith with no credit rating with God. From creation to Christ, love precedes us, embraces us, and motivates us.

One of the confessions of my own faith tradition has it that "We believe and confess the canonical Scriptures of the holy prophets and apostles of both Testaments to be the true Word of God and to have sufficient authority of themselves, not of (human beings)."[5] Though it is true that the Apostle Paul in Galatians 3:24–26 made reference to the Law as a disciplinarian until Christ came, ending as a disciplinarian now that Christ has come, this can be misconstrued. Just as Jesus in Matthew was reinterpreting the Law, and Matthew was centering Israel's story around a new lawgiver, Paul was interpreting how the Law was to be understood in the church of Jesus Christ. Neither advocated that the Law should be done away with, nor that it wasn't from God, "holy, just, and good" (Rom 7:12).

I conclude this lengthy grappling section with an Old Testament story in hope that our views of a healthy appreciation of both testaments may be confirmed or improved. This is the reconciliation between Esau and Jacob (Gen 32–33).

After being away for twenty years, Jacob returns to his homeland near the territory of his brother Esau. I must pause to say that the narrative is itself so rich that a summary of the story cannot do it justice. Nonetheless, Jacob's messengers, whom he had sent ahead to take Esau's temperature, report that Esau "is coming to meet you, and four hundred men are with him" (Gen 32:6).

Jacob's venture with God and his anxiety about returning to face Esau are packed into this prayer: "O God of my father Abraham and God of my father Isaac, O Lord who said to me, 'Return to your country and to your kindred, and I will do you good,' I am not worthy of the least of all the

---

5. *Book of Confessions*, 5.001.

steadfast love and all the faithfulness you have shown your servant, for with only my staff I crossed the Jordan; and now I have become two companies. Deliver me, please, from the hand of my brother, from the hand of Esau, for I am afraid of him; he may come and kill us all, the mothers with the children. Yet you have said, 'I will surely do you good, and make your offspring as the sand of the sea, which cannot be counted because of their number'" (Gen 32:9–12).

Jacob then proceeds to orchestrate a succession of droves of animals with a certain distance between each, all as gifts for Esau. "For Jacob thought, 'I may appease Esau with the present that goes ahead of me, and afterwards I shall see his face; perhaps he will accept me'" (Gen 32:20). Implicit in this is Jacob's contrition for stealing Esau's birthright.

Following this, Jacob crosses the River Jabbok with his wives, maids, children and possessions. Wherever exactly he remains in relation to them, "Jacob was left alone; and a man wrestled with him until daybreak" (Gen 32:24). What ensues is the struggle with the night messenger, the wounding of Jacob's hip, the divine blessing and the name change to "Israel," which means "God strives." Under the cover of darkness, all is quite mysterious.

Next day Jacob rises with the dawn, limping because of his hip. He names the place Peniel, literally, "the face of God," "because I have seen the face of God and yet my life is preserved" (Gen 32:30–31).

On to Esau, before whom Jacob repeatedly bows himself to the ground. But Esau comes running, embraces him, and falls upon his neck and kisses him, and they weep.

Esau says, "What do you mean by all this company I have met?"

Jacob replies, "To find favor with my lord." Notice how the younger son now treats the older with exquisite respect.

The dialogue is poignant. "But Esau said, 'I have enough, my brother; keep what you have for yourself.'

"Jacob said, 'No, please; if I find favor with you, then accept my present from my hand; for truly to see your face is like seeing the face of God—since you have received me with such favor'" (Gen 33:4–11).

Jacob left home years before under a cloud of murderous threat. Now, he returns to see in his brother's face, the very face of God.

Divine favor accompanies Jacob on the run and voices itself when he pillows his head on the stone at Bethel. Through a difficult twenty years with Laban, through the night of his woundedness and blessing, to the daylight of seeing God in his brother's face, Jacob eventually basks in divine acceptance. "Esau ran to meet him, and embraced him, and fell on his neck and kissed him, and they wept" (Gen 33:4). What majestic story of Jesus echoes this?

The Old Testament adumbrates the New in its picture of alienation and reconciliation. Divine favor accompanies the characters who must find in their woundedness a change of heart, even a broken heart, that breaks open to the pursuing grace of God's lasting embrace.

CHAPTER FIVE

In Our Need

As we look at the story of God with Us through Matthew's eyes, we see Jesus through the lens of a healer. Immediately following the Sermon on the Mount, chapters 8 and 9 offer a series of signs of the kingdom. I put it that way, following the New Testament scholar, Martin Dibelius.

Dibelius makes clear that the healing miracles of the Gospels are directly related to Jesus' proclamation of the kingdom of God. By contrast to miracle stories around Asclepius, the Greek physician, "in the case of Jesus' cures, one must think of entirely different and quite special psychical [meaning pychosomatic] factors. The oldest accounts [meaning those the author attributes to the earthly life of Jesus, not later] do not tell of a miracle worker, who performs as many miracles as possible, but of the proclaimer and guarantor of the coming Kingdom of God; God himself is drawing near to the world, and his nearness is perceived in the fact that through Jesus he speaks, through him he acts, through him he heals."[1]

When John was in prison and sent his disciples to ask if Jesus was the one to come or "shall we seek another," Jesus says this to them: "Go and tell John what you hear and see: the blind receive their sight, the lame walk, the lepers are cleansed, the deaf hear, the dead are raised, and the poor have good news brought to them. And blessed is anyone who takes no offense at me" (Matt 11:4–6). John was asking Jesus about his role as the Messiah, and Jesus offered signs of the kingdom.

Though it is understandable that modern readers may miss the references, what was clear to Jews of Jesus' day was a passage like Isaiah 61:1–4, "The Spirit of the Lord God is upon me . . ." Jesus read that from the scroll

---

1. Dibelius, *Jesus*, 83.

in the synagogue in Nazareth, according to Luke 4:18–19. The messianic age, the coming kingdom, and good news for the oppressed are related in a changing weather front. Signs of the kingdom, such as healings and exorcisms, are like the telltale clouds of an eerie calm or an evening sunset. As Dibelius asserts, Jesus was not merely in the business of healing as many as he could. What he said and did was part and parcel of the kingdom days that John the Baptist anticipated.

In a passage, quite profound in a pastoral sense, Dibelius writes, "Suffering, including physical suffering, is a characteristic mark of this world; only God's Kingdom will show once more the finished creation, untouched by pain. Jesus' cures do not signify an arbitrary anticipation of this Kingdom, which no man knows when God will send. On the contrary, they signify the proclamation and promise of this Kingdom; they prove that it is on the way, that God through the One whom he has sent is already permitting the splendor of the Kingdom to shine out here and there."[2]

Two observations: one, it is the person and work of Jesus that represents, even embodies, God, such that Matthew's main theme can comfortably be "God with Us." And two, there is an urgency related to what God was doing through Jesus.

We read in Matthew the rather testy way that Jesus speaks about the towns of Chorazin, Bethsaida and Capernaum which will be judged harshly for not responding to his works (Matt 11:20–24). We read in Matthew about the children of the kingdom who will be cast out and punished (Matt 8:12). And I confess that I flinch at words such as "outer darkness" and "weeping and gnashing of teeth" (More on them later). Nonetheless, I emphasize again that these are the harsh words of a Jewish prophet spoken like a Jeremiah to God's disobedient people Israel. They are not anti-Semitic any more than the prophets of old were.

As we continue to travel with Matthew, we need to keep in mind the context of conflict that led to Jesus' death. Those who could not see the new work of God in him were missing out. At the same time, I draw upon the words of Jesus from the cross in Luke, "Father, forgive them, for they know not what they are doing" (Luke 23:24). Matthew's Jesus is embroiled in an intense argument. Luke's Jesus offers more perspective and extends a father's invitation to the elder brother (Luke 15). Paul offers the most theological discussion of God's call and promise to Israel that God will not take back (Rom. 9–11).

All the same, we see in Jesus among the poor, the sick, and the demon-possessed the very heart of God. "Then Jesus went about all the cities and

---

2. Dibelius, *Jesus*, 87.

villages, teaching in their synagogues, and proclaiming the good news of the kingdom, and curing every disease and every sickness. When he saw the crowds, he had compassion for them, because they were harassed and helpless, like sheep without a shepherd" (Matt 9:35–36).

The story that Matthew advances is one of proclamation of the kingdom evidenced in good news for the poor and compassionate touch for those who are suffering. In Jesus, God feels for those most lost, whom others overlook as outcast. His is a gathering ministry that begins with Israel and extends to the world. This is both why he limits himself, at first, to the lost sheep of the house of Israel, but will not withhold God's power and presence from a Canaanite woman (Matt 15) and later all the nations to the close of the age (Matt 28).

An Imploring Canaanite and a Gruff Jesus

Matthew, following Mark, takes Jesus to the region of Tyre and Sidon, over to the Mediterranean coast from Galilee and up towards modern-day Lebanon. Mark has it that "he entered a house and did not want anyone to know that he was there" (Mark 7:24). Matthew says, "Just then a Canaanite woman from that region came out and started shouting, 'Have mercy on me, Lord, Son of David'" (Matt 15:22).

What follows in Matthew is an intense and moving dialogue. When the woman makes her appeal to Jesus on behalf of her daughter, tortured by a demon, "Jesus did not answer her a word" (Matt 15:23). The silence of Jesus in Matthew shouts something. We are not sure what, at first.

Apparently the woman, ignored by Jesus, goes after his disciples, because they say to Jesus, in effect, "She is pestering us," "Send her away." But rather than send her away, he keeps the dialogue going by saying, "I was sent only to the lost sheep of the house of Israel."

Despite which, the woman prostrates herself at Jesus' feet. "Lord, help me," she issues a second deep cry.

Matthew evokes the reader's response. By now, most of us are not sympathizing with Jesus or the disciples.

It gets worse when Jesus says, "It is not fair to take the children's food and throw it to the dogs" (Matt 15:26). Ouch!

But she is not put off. "Yes, Lord, yet even the dogs eat the crumbs that fall from their master's table" (Matt 15:27). The Canaanite woman never oversteps though she is desperately persistent.

Jesus is finally overcome. "'O woman, great is your faith! Let it be done for you as you wish.' And her daughter was healed instantly" (Matt 15:28).

Though Mark tells the same story, Matthew resets it with exquisite dialogue. I imagine this incident actually occurred because there is no effort by either evangelist to put make-up on Jesus. He doesn't look good in this story.

Clearly the star of the story is the foreigner from a Jewish point of view. She does not veer from her intent to save her daughter. She is willing to be ridiculed on account of her greater purpose.

Jesus first refuses to acknowledge the woman without even a nod her way. When the disciples implore him to get rid of her, he merely lectures. "I was sent only to the lost sheep of the house of Israel." Then it gets ugly. "It is not fair to take bread from the children's table and to throw it to dogs"

Though we might rather excise this story from the gospels, why did Matthew take Mark's version and add acid to it? Here are a few guesses.

Jesus had already sent the Twelve out on a mission only to "the lost sheep of the house of Israel" (Matt 10:6). These are the same exact words as 15: 24. He is keeping precedent with his own stated commission of the Twelve. Matthew alone uses this phrase: "the lost sheep of the house of Israel."

From a literary point of view, Matthew establishes a precedent likely following Jesus himself. I refer to the literary Matthew and how Jesus, even when he has gone away to Gentile territory, his whereabouts not to be known, does not embrace the Gentiles there. That fact runs counter to the overall theme of Jesus in Matthew which is more than favorable to Gentiles.

Remember, this Gospel includes the Gentiles from the beginning with the light that draws the magi from the east to Bethlehem. And it concludes with Jesus' commission to disciples to teach "all nations." More often than not, "nations" in Scripture refers to the Gentile world.

Now, with a Gentile woman at his feet, imploring him for her daughter's life, Jesus gives both precedent to his mission to Jews first and struggles in the passage with the great faith he finds before him. The effect is to show us the one who did not come "to abolish the law but to fulfill it" (Matt 5:17), and how he reinterprets the law to apply it in a way that includes Gentiles.

In other words, we see in this passage the working out of Matthew's Gospel as Jesus moves from within Judaism only to serve also as a light to the nations (Isa 49:6). Previously, I mentioned tensions within Scripture. Between Isaiah chapters 40–55 and Ezra/Nehemiah, we see two versions of Jewish faith, one with Israel in a role as light to the nations, and the other, with Israel resetting a strict obedience involving racial, religious, and ritual purity. What we see in Matthew's Jesus is not a Jew leaving Judaism behind, but a Jewish prophet, like Isaiah, venturing toward the horizon of an ancient vision.

The geographical move from Galilee to Tyre sets the stage of the story. Furthermore, it accents the movement of the story while acknowledging the tension of two visions that abide both Jesus' ministry and the new community of faith Matthew addresses.

Turning to the woman herself, we see in her an extraordinary example of one who reaches out to Jesus from her deep need. Despite everything aligned against her, including Jesus himself, she cries out for mercy to the Son of David. This reminds us of two other persons in the Gospels: blind Bartimaeus in Mark 10 and the man born blind in John 9. Each moves from the pain he knows to the light he seeks. Though not blind, the Canaanite woman shows faith, not by profession, but by action.

She was a foreigner to Israel. Therefore, she was outside the bounds of the racial, religious, and ritual purity code. She was a woman whose gender was regarded as inferior in much of the ancient world. The Samaritan woman at the well in John 4 comes to mind. Yet, Jesus says, "O woman, your faith is great." This is a kind of beatitude, a pronouncement of God's favor.

In Matthew, Jesus is embroiled in stretching Israel's bounds through the proclamation of God's kingdom for all. This sign of the kingdom shines on a foreigner whom God receives in mercy. Once before in Matthew, a Gentile centurion's servant was healed. Now, a Canaanite woman, called a "dog," becomes herself a sign of the kingdom and of what God with Us will do before this Gospel has run its course.

I know of no more powerful encounter wherein our hero Jesus struggles with the boundaries drawn around Israel and defers to the cries of this Canaanite woman of great faith. In one brief story we read and feel God's mission breaking open.

Hope and Grapple

Wherever I have discussed human need as our access to God, I have met with a certain kind of resistance. I have also met that resistance in myself. It is hard to accept that we are powerless over certain forces, trends, facts of life. As a result, we have padded the mind with positive attitudes and views of divine blessing that run counter to the gospel story itself.

Professor Kate Bowler of Duke Divinity School has made an exquisite study of this resistance to the gospel story. She calls its manifestation in modern America the "Prosperity Gospel." The title of her most popular book says a lot: *Everything Happens for a Reason and Other Lies I've Loved*.

By way of a poignant coincidence, her life has become one of the major texts of her scholarly work. Living among and studying communities who equated prayer and confession with tickets of admission to God's grace, she found herself with an awful diagnosis of colon cancer.

She writes, 'In a spiritual world in which healing is a divine right, illness a symptom of unconfessed sin—a symptom of a lack of forgiveness, unfaithfulness, unexamined attitudes, or careless words . . . I felt like faithlessness personified."[3] Bowler explores views reminiscent of Job's friends whereby achievement and wealth are signs of God's answers to prayer and special blessing. In a similar vein, she tells of people at funerals who pray at coffins, expecting the dead to rise.[4] In this scheme, illness, poverty, and death itself are affronts to true faith.

The keen insight of Bowler's work is to recognize such views as a kind of theodicy.[5] This is one way of justifying the wrong of the world in relation to the goodness and blessings of God. More than that, Bowler will not leave the rest of us alone, because she recognizes that within us all there is at least a wish that God will, not someday, but now, clear the debris from the landscape of life.

Who of us has not fantasized that advanced heart disease, diagnoses of Alzheimers, not to mention human greed and our penchant for conflict, will fade into the sunset? My question is more flippant than Bowler's strong sympathy with those of us who desire that our loved ones or we ourselves survive and improve, and that the world be a better place for our children and grandchildren.

It is a hard pill to swallow when Jesus says, "Those who want to save their life will lose it, and those who lose their life for my sake will find it" (Matt 16:25). More to the point, the great story of God with Us in Matthew and the rest of the New Testament is about a savior who pursued the way of the cross and offered his life to God and for the world rather than take up the mantle of a messiah who would neither suffer nor die.

Those who want to begin the story with the resurrection ignore all that precedes it and how scandalous it was, even to the disciples themselves. "Get behind me, Satan," were Jesus' words to Peter who rebuked him for imagining that he would suffer and die (Matt 16:21–23).

What Bowler does so well is to show how certain views of theodicy are not to better understand the ways of God but to control the ways of God that make us so uncomfortable. Rather, losing one's life to gain it is about living into a paradox that God makes possible but which controlling reason cannot perceive.

3. Bowler, *Everything Happens*, 16.
4. Bowler, *Everything Happens*, 34–35.
5. Bowler, *Everything Happens*, 123.

I have spent many hours in a parents' support group for those of us who have children struggling with or recovering from addiction. I have turned my theological eye to the Twelve Steps of Alcoholics Anonymous and concluded that to live into recovery, we must accept the paradox of recovery.

The first step is to acknowledge that we are powerless over the disease of alcoholism. The second is to turn one's life over to a higher power, however one conceives of such. What follows is a scheme of steps to take.

If one is powerless, how can he or she take any steps into recovery? Is the very foundation of AA not a contradiction? Yes, it is. But it is, nonetheless, true. Its truth is borne out by all those who have lived by it and discovered new life in hope.

AA's paradox is the same as the Christian paradox. We must surrender ourselves to the grace of God. And then we must follow in the way of Jesus. We are powerless and yet taking steps. We cannot save ourselves, and yet we extend our hands to one who can save.

God's grace and human freedom represent a tension which is a contradiction to the controlling devices of an inflexible reason. But countless millions attest that by God's grace, we are freed for life. Only by admitting that I am powerless over addiction, mortality, harpies of the mind, and oppressions such as greed, poverty, racism, and violence can I begin to find life and ways to grapple in hope that God is yet with us. Love has not abandoned us. The great story yet embraces us and forwards us.

Can I understand all the ins and outs of it? No, I cannot. But have I known its power even through dark nights of the soul? Yes. Do I believe that sickness, death, and evil cut across this mortal landscape and seem, many times, to rule it? Yes, I see that fact of life as clearly as the next person.

Nonetheless, God has come among us as a lover, suffering all the hazards of any ventured love, dying by the hands of forces aligned against the very heart of love. Were we able to control love, we might somehow feel padded and protected from life's rough edges and terrible slices, but is love controlled still love? The question leads us to the choice of faith, to make our best effort to control everything, or to surrender ourselves to the gracious rule of a holy love. "Faith, hope, and love," these three abide, "and the greatest of these is love" (1 Cor. 13:13.). That path alone takes us to God.

CHAPTER SIX

Fragmentation and Reduction

IRONICALLY THE MODERN CHURCH can serve as an example of an unstoried life. Years ago I felt the push/pull of disparate demands and tasks. The process of getting the weekly sermon and service together is an enjoyable one for me as are other aspects of ministry, but it is the compounding and pressure of various tasks, rolling like an unstemmed tide, that can lead to trouble.

Not only are there pastoral concerns which do not follow a schedule, there are committee meetings to staff. These are related to the variety of programs in a given congregation or parish: worship, education, youth, stewardship, budget, building and grounds, to name areas of work that draw a pastor or priest's attention. In many ways, the work of the rabbi or the imam is quite similar.

Most clergy also relate to judicatories, ecumenical/interfaith bodies, and community service organizations. These entail boards and committees as well.

We should never underestimate that clergy have families and friends which need their time and attention. These involve the usual matters of children, schools, bills, and occasional sickness, not to mention devotion to these special relationships, developing and repairing them.

As one feels dissipated from time to time, faith can lose its focus while busyness (as in, not getting around to everything) leaves theological reflection on the shelf. Ministry itself can put distance between clergy and the resources that nourish them.

Though our intellectual and emotional lives are not so divided as some imagine, my experience is that we first feel the drain of a fragmented life. As a kind of spiritual discipline, we must find our way to think about faith again. But under the weight of so much to do and feeling pulled apart at the core, those called upon to affirm their faith publicly on a regular basis may be lightning rods of what is happening to the society at large.

"Where is the life we have lost in living?" are T.S. Eliot's words which speak to the mind and heart together.[1] What sense can we make of why we in the church or other houses of worship are called to do what we do? I have thought of this as a blur of vocation, not yet a loss of faith, but a nagging sense that all we are doing does not much matter.

Which leads to the question, "Is there any way in which writing prayers and drafting budgets, preparing a study of Jeremiah, and sitting on the steeple repair task force cohere?" I am not saying that clergy do all of these. There are many who participate. But when asking, "What does all this mean?," organizational efficiency loses priority for the questioning spirit. If there's nothing to this, then working harder or more efficiently doesn't matter.

What is the problem? Admittedly there are several interrelated components. But if one cannot focus on a compelling reason for what one does and who one is doing it, a day off, counseling, spiritual guidance will not, by themselves, get us back on track, and this is not to disparage any of these (and other) important remedies.

The great essayist and mystery writer G.K. Chesterton once involved his detective, Father Brown, in a curious murder investigation. A foreigner, a well-known poet, was accused of killing a neighbor. He, the foreigner, called upon the man found dead, but knocking on the door to no answer, presumed the man hadn't yet returned from a professional dinner.

Rather than return to his house, the poet waited in the expansive front garden of his neighbor. There he was found, having been waiting for two hours, while the judge, whom he had called upon, lay dead, murdered, his head issuing blood into a pond in the back garden. Without an alibi, the poet was indicted for the murder and put on trial.

Father Brown, who had been staying in the neighborhood, got drawn into the investigation on the day of the murder. Weeks later, when the poet went on trial, the cleric attended the courtroom, curious about what he thought were loose ends in the case. One present difficulty for the poet was his refusal to say in the witness box what he was doing for those two unaccounted hours in the front garden while a man was being murdered out back. As a result, the prosecuting attorney began to make a rather outrageous argument based solely on fear of foreigners, and that all England

---

1. Eliot, *Complete Poems and Plays*, 96.

might suffer the same murderous fate were this man not hanged for his dastardly deed.

Father Brown, aware of the accused man's reputation as a poet, began to mount another argument for his possible innocence. He had found a delightful place out of sight with an inspiring vantage point to compose verse in his head for those two unexplained hours. In a strange land, he felt uncomfortable owning up to the fact that he was turning words over in his mind as someone met their end. In Chesterton's wry way, he raised the current problem of prejudice against foreigners and coupled it with the common misunderstanding about the vocation of the man on trial who had rather be thought a murderer than a poet.[2]

In many very practical circles, the truth that we are struggling with a sense of meaning and purpose can get buried. It is thought to be a luxury we cannot afford compared to so many greater needs. Some who do not engage life by trying to make sense of it may possess more understanding for carpenters, gardeners, and engineers, even criminals, than those with a theological bent. Clergy, like poets, can struggle to explain what they do to those with very hands-on minds. I must catch myself here and not limit questions of meaning and purpose to clergy. There are many within the church and without who wrestle with such thoughts.

Why such awkwardness about discussing them? The magic-minded Blaise Pascal once asked, "How comes it that a cripple does not offend us, but a fool does? Because a cripple recognizes that we walk straight, but a fool declares that we are silly."[3] In a similar vein, how is it that someone with a broken leg is no threat to my mind? Because when I see someone with a broken leg, I do not worry that I might have one. It is not the same with how well our minds and hearts hold together. A fool can raise self-doubt among us, like the fool on the heath with King Lear. Dementia in others can cause us to question the hold we have on our wits. A number of people had rather just assume all is well in hand because raising questions can surface doubts, not only about faith, but about our grip on reality.

The question I am raising is this: How can we cope with the fragmentation of our lives that pulls us apart at the core? It is a question that cannot be satisfied by more of anything, more money, more prestige, more acquaintances, more experiences. If no great story serves as a framework or a narrative for our lives, we can collapse within. Padding the surface against the sharp edges of existence cannot heal a hidden anxiousness related to the lack of any sacred coherence.

2. Chesterton, *Complete Father Brown*, 467–482.
3. Blaise Pascal, *Pensees*, 23.

Compassion for the Harassed and Helpless Among Us and Within

"When Jesus saw the crowds, he had compassion for them, because they were harassed and helpless, like sheep without a shepherd" (Matt 9: 36) This reading of the crowd came upon the heels of Jesus preaching the good news of the kingdom, and curing diseases and other ailments. In other words, he was among them.

I wonder about God with Us today walking among our many needs. Do we not also appear harassed by many things and helpless as sheep scattered by lightning bolts and claps of thunder?

What I have just done is to juxtapose a background story from Matthew and the foreground of our lives as we are pushed and pulled in many directions at once. Background and foreground are concepts used in composing film scenes. Along with a middleground, the interplay of these visual distances is employed by the film director and cinematographer to offer a kind of texture for the eye and mind.

Orson Welles and his camera genuis, Gregg Toland, composed the film Citizen Kane to show background, middleground, and foreground at once with equal clarity. The technique had been used before, but Welles and Toland raised it to an art form.

What it does is show an interrelatedness of characters, action, and setting by allowing one to affect the other(s). The eye and the mind of the audience then go to work on what is before them and somehow bring them together at the suggestion of the filmmakers. What comes together for viewers is not only an aesthetic sense as if a scene were merely pleasing to the eye. Rather, the eye and the mind work in tandem to harvest intelligible sense from a story portrayed before them.

Most films, of course, employ the words of a narrator or dialogue of the characters. Needless to say, I am not underestimating the value of verbal storytelling. But the power of film as a visual medium has been the interplay of images by a variety of technical methods to suggest meanings. Here I am drawing a comparison with the interplay of ancient biblical texts in their contexts and ourselves as modern characters. This is another kind of background, foreground, and middleground, portrayed in the great story of scripture that holds them together and brings them into focus.

Though this comparison may, at first, seem out of focus, I suggest that we think about the actual, not metaphorical, function of the eye itself. Unless we have had a problem seeing, we can take our vision for granted. As I look out my window at the house across the street, I normally do not wonder what my eyes are doing to bring it into focus. But when I also look at a notebook open about twenty inches before me on the table, I realize that my eyes have to adjust from the brightness of the day outside where they have been focusing to this darker room and what is written on the page on the near table. Though I don't usually pause to think about the adjustments my eyes are making, they are doing so all the time.

In the same sense, we are taking in the world around us and loosely putting it together in our minds. Not until we begin to articulate what we have been perceiving do we become aware of what coheres or what may be thousands of loose ends. As with our actual vision, there may be no reason for us to reflect on what is happening until cataracts develop or a retina tears. Fragmentation with its push and pull of us as communities and individuals can surface questions about the worth of all that we are doing and, of course, our own worth.

Helping us to hold background and foreground together, the biblical story and stories figure into how we compose the world. Scripture speaks to our delights and joys, confusion and suffering, great expectations that excite us or the heavy weight of too much time on our hands. But we have long since passed a time when reading the Bible was our only or even the main source for modern living, if it ever was.

We find ourselves confused by a welter of offers for our hearts and minds. A perusal of the self-help section in the few remaining bookstores, what comes to us online, or a tour of Sunday morning television is simply dizzying. In a consumer society, I think of this as the bidding war for the soul.

To help navigate all that's on offer, I have been guided by the Canadian philosopher Charles Taylor. In his work, *Sources of the Self: The Making of the Modern Identity*, he is not merely concerned about a person or self being constituted by doing right and wrong. As important as that is, Taylor explores an authentic self, we might say, by focusing on the question, "What makes life worth living?"[4]

This phrase gets at what he is up to and speaks to our traveling with Matthew. Taylor writes, "So while it may not be judged a moral lapse that I am living a life that is not really worthwhile or fulfilling, to describe me in these terms is nevertheless to condemn me in the name of a standard, independent of my own tastes and desires, which I ought to acknowledge."[5] Taylor's overall purpose is in asking, "What source(s) is there, greater than ourselves, that truly makes sense of who we are?"

---

4. Taylor, *Sources of the Self*, 4.
5. Taylor, *Sources of the Self*, 4.

Over many years in ministry I have heard parents say, "I want the kids to go to church school to learn the difference between right and wrong." Setting aside the question, "What role do parents have in teaching right and wrong?" I inwardly hang my head when I hear this. The purpose of the church is much greater than a school of morals in the limited sense often meant.

Matthew, Mark, and Luke get at it when Jesus says, "If any want to become my followers, let them deny themselves and take up their cross and follow me. For those who want to save their life will lose it, and those who lose their life for my sake will find it. For what will it profit them if they gain the whole world but forfeit their life? Or what will they give in return for their life?" (Matt 16:24–26). There is something great and ultimate about Jesus' words.

Though some want to contextualize them carefully in the first century world, why wouldn't Jesus be talking more generally about the value of a life, a life's worthwhileness, we might say? As I hinted earlier, we can offer many candidates for modern efforts to "gain the whole world." Making oneself better is part and parcel of American culture, and I value that, but taken by themselves, achievement and success are like eating food that does not nourish.

Following Jesus in the Gospel passage above implies a certain orientation to life, shaped by a certain story. Though most of us do not carry the cross in the sense of going to our death on account of the choice we have made to follow Jesus, following is, nonetheless, going against the grain of choices that by themselves lead to death and nothing more.

This is where I want to return to the work of Charles Taylor and relate to it my view of fragmentation as it dissipates the "What for?" or "Why does it matter?" of a life. In a masterful thread of intellectual history, Taylor shows how moral reasoning has gotten separated from a view of the good, as in Plato, or God, as in the Judeo-Christian Scriptures.

Once there is no "out there," a compelling reality that invites our attention, our obedience, our lives to move forward, then we are thrown back upon our own resources. Through a complex of developments, morality has been handed over to "rational agents" who by their own criteria determine what is good, valuable, right, and wrong.

Taylor says, "The work I am embarked upon here [in *Sources*] could be called in large degree an essay in retrieval."[6] Retrieval from what? It is a modern assumption by sophisticated persons that there is no evidence, no reliable sources for determining what a life is by ancient lights. Plato

---

6. Taylor, *Sources of the Self*, 10.

and Scripture, the world religions have nothing to recommend them. All we know of life is what can be proven by scientific experiments or what awaits to be proven. This "reductionistic" view, as it is called, is so by virtue of limiting what we can know to what can be proven by the methods of modern science.

At the same time, Taylor observes that the same folk who have discounted the ancient sources "are all universalists now about respect for life and . . . that [means] we believe it would be utterly wrong and unfounded to draw boundaries any narrower than around the whole human race."[7]

Of course, this view is admirable. But on what is it based other than a criteria that presumably they have thought up themselves? Jesus, speaking about building a foundation on the sand in Matthew, comes to mind (Matt 7:26). Taylor has carefully shown that "respect for the life of the whole human race" is composed of many threads woven over time. That all humans are created in God's image (Genesis 1:26) and that "God so loved the world (John 3:16)" are significant blocks in the foundation, threads in the tapestry of life's worth.

A myriad of other materials are on offer in this bidding war for life's true value, that is, something on which we can stand firm. But will they endure? And can they uphold us? The fragmentation of modern life blurs our attention to what lasts. The reduction of useful knowledge to what can be proven in the lab starves our hearts and minds as to what nourishes them.

Hope and Grapple

Kafka's short story, "A Hunger Artist," has intrigued me ever since I read it in college. Briefly, it is set in a day when the side show act of a man going without food is quite popular. Crowds gather day after day before the cage where he exhibits himself. By night, watchers are hired to make sure that he does not cheat. The hunger artist is so committed to his craft that the proprietors have to place a limit of forty days on him, lest he starve himself.

But as time goes by, interest in the hunger artist wanes. His venue becomes a side show to the side show with most folk passing him by to see "the menagerie of animals." The circus managers cease keeping track of him. By this time, he has starved himself well beyond the once appointed limit.

"Poking in the straw of a cage that they thought was no longer in use, they found the man." "Are you still fasting? . . . When on earth do you mean to stop?"

---

7. Taylor, *Sources of the Self*, 6–7.

The hunger artist responds in a weak whisper to the ear of the overseer who has drawn close to hear, "I have to fast, I can't help it."

"And why can't you help it?"

"Because I couldn't find the food I liked. If I had found it, believe me, I should have made no fuss and stuffed myself like you or anyone else."[8]

As many churches of North America began to lose their members in the 1970s, we ramped up our efforts to stave our losses. Were we out-of-step with the trends? Were we otherwise somehow irrelevant? Major studies were undertaken.

We had to understand the dynamics of the corporate, program, mid-size, and small church. We had to be clearer as to who we are in a certain place and time. Each congregation or parish had to identify its mission in a brief statement catchy enough for every member to recite it before bedtime.

Generation theory came on another wave. If congregations cannot meet the special, studied needs of each generation, we will lose them. How many congregations and parishes went to contemporary services? How many had to return to one or two?

All the while, stewardship campaigns became more and more glitzy. We were taught and told that this was not merely fundraising. It has a theological foundation. No doubt it does, but "meeting the needs of the saints" does not always translate into paying larger staff salaries and steeple repairs.

To get us back on track, some suggested that we needed to teach discipleship, not membership. "The church is not a social club," was spoken as if we gray heads had never heard it before

I must confess that older clergy, perhaps feeling the sting of decline on our watch, spoke under our breath about the young gurus. "Did they think we had never read Bonhoeffer, not to mention Jesus Christ?" In an age of rapid change and diminishing numbers, grumbling can become the undercurrent of church life.

Yet, even when the church was burgeoning in numbers just after WWII, some prescient thinkers cautioned against our raison d'etre giving way to building expansion and programs for all. In 1959, the theologian Joseph Sittler bemoaned professional fundraising with such "well oiled unction that [it] would have glazed the eyeballs of Saint Paul."[9]

What I am saying is that we Americans, being Americans, go at everything as if by identifying any problem, we can somehow fix it. When trends go our way, we take the credit. I heard once of a burgeoning congregation that put the five keys to its growth on the front page of the weekly bulletin.

---

8. Kafka, *Selected Stories*, 200.

9. Sittler, *Grace Notes*, 80–81.

Not one among them noted the fact that this church was located in one of the fastest growing suburbs in the whole country. After WWII, we could not take credit for amazing church growth due to the nation's rush to normality after years of war. For all our efforts to salvage our losses since, we may not deserve blame for change on a massive scale that is beyond our control. As when a town loses the single industry that has employed so much of its population, local churches cannot simply replace their losses with clever programming.

The point I am grappling with is about the food itself, the bread of life. However we package and deliver it, what if we cannot create an appetite for it? As with the hunger artist, times have changed. Those attracted to what went before have passed us by for other venues. To state this baldly, I am concerned that doing things better may not be enough to supply all the wants of our society. Are we too distracted to take notice of deeper needs within?

We live in a time when people can be both malnourished and overweight. So full of what is on offer, we may not want what truly nourishes the human spirit. "One does not live by bread alone, but by every word that comes from the mouth of God" (Matt 4:4).

Careful now. I am not ignoring human wholeness, and our need for bodily nourishment and spiritual food, social justice, and lifting our hearts to God. Instead, I am calling our attention to the American can-do spirit. Sometimes practical and roll-up-your-sleeves methods neither apply to overwhelming trends nor to the mysteries of God and creation.

There will always be an appetite in our society for the impressive. There will always be good people who volunteer to help as they can. God bless them! But there is something other than what immediately catches our attention and what we can fix by our smarts and muscle. Sometimes we need an old kind of faithfulness that keeps digging around in the straw of our existence for a hunger that is nourished by another kind of bread. Through our ups and downs, who will bear witness to that? I'm just saying.

CHAPTER SEVEN

Jesus, the Message, and the People

WHEN JESUS WENT UP on the mountain in Matthew's Gospel, the story likens him to a new Moses. Moses went up on the mountain (Horeb or Sinai) to receive the Torah, or the Ten Commandments, on tablets of stone (Exod 20). Down below the people were encamped before the mountain, seeing God settled upon it, indicated by "thundering and lightning, a thick cloud and a trumpet blast" (Exod 19).

God, Moses, the Law, and Israel are masterfully placed in a kind of theological positioning. God's presence is powerful and paramount in Exodus. Moses is God's voice to the people. But "when all the people witnessed the thundering and the lightning, the sound of the trumpet and the mountain smoking, they were afraid and trembled and stood at a distance, and said to Moses, 'You speak to us, and we will listen, but do not let God speak to us, or we will die'" (Exod 19:18–19).

No question, Moses occupies an intermediary role between God and the people. Matthew evokes the awesome nature of the role that Moses occupied but later distinguishes Jesus from Moses and Elijah on the mountain of transfiguration (Matt 17). Yet, it is with the impact of a Moses in interpreting "the law and the prophets" that Jesus speaks to the people. "Now when Jesus had finished saying these things, the crowds were astounded at his teaching, for he taught them as one having authority and not as their scribes" (Matt 7:28–29).

Before God on the holy mountain, the multitude who heard God's words through the voice of Moses were made a people. In a covenanting ceremony, Moses "rose early in the morning, and built an altar at the foot of the mountain . . . He sent young men of the people of Israel, who offered burnt offerings and sacrificed oxen as offerings of well-being to the Lord. Moses took half of the blood and put it in a basin, and half of the blood he dashed against the altar. Then he took the book of the covenant [Exodus 21–24, a collection of laws combining interpretations of the Ten Commandments and additional cultic regulations] and read it in the hearing of the people; and they said, 'All that the Lord has spoken we will do, and we will be obedient.' Moses took the blood and dashed it on the people and said, 'See the blood of the covenant that the Lord has made with you in accordance with all these words'" (Exod 24:4–8).

The notes from *The New Oxford Annotated Bible* on this passage are significant. "The ritual dramatizes the uniting of the two parties: the Lord, whose presence is represented by the altar, and the people . . . The blood of the covenant (Matt 26:28; 1 Cor 11:25) reflects the ancient view that blood was efficacious in establishing community between God and human beings."[1]

I quote these passages at some length to raise a question. In the Sermon on the Mount, we see Jesus, God with Us, whom Matthew styles a new Moses. We hear Jesus' emphasis on the Law. "I have not come to abolish the law and the prophets but to fulfill" (Matt 5:17). But where are the people, and what is their role in Matthew's theological configuration?

I suggest that the implied, later stated (Matt 26:28; Mark 14:24), blood of the covenant points to the new creation of a people. Alternative ancient texts actually include the word "new" before "covenant" in Matthew and Mark. Luke, in fact, includes it (Luke 22:20) as does Paul (1 Cor. 11:25).

Throughout Matthew, as we have already observed, there is Jesus reaching out to Gentiles, the centurion (Matt 8), the Canaanite woman (Matt 15, though reluctantly), tax collectors and sinners (Matt 9). From the beginning, the Gentile magi journey to his birth (Matt 2), and to the horizon of time, Jesus commissions his disciples "to make disciples of all nations" (Matt 28; 'nations" refers to the world of the Gentiles).

All the while, Jesus is reinterpreting the law and the prophets in a way that eschews the narrow ceremonial laws and opens the law to Jews and Gentiles who are not racially, religiously, and ritually pure. We read this most clearly in Matthew 15 where Jesus says, "Listen and understand: it is not what goes into the mouth that defiles a person, but it is what comes out of the mouth that defiles" (Matt 15:11). This was spoken in reference to the Pharisees and scribes asking, "Why do your disciples break the tradition of the elders? For they do not wash their hands before they eat" (Matt 15:1–2).

We cannot know for sure who the crowd were who heard the Sermon on the Mount. But in Galilee among ordinary people, they were likely not

---

1. *New Oxford Annotated Bible*, 101.

a gathering of those Jews who kept the ceremonial laws most rigorously. When we look at the rigor of Jesus' reinterpretation of the law in Matthew 5, I will make some comments about Pharisees and ordinary Jews of that day. At this point, let's recognize that Jesus in Matthew is clear to make a distinction between what we may call the Ten Commandments and all the regulations of the ceremonial law around them.

As I have said before, in Matthew 15:19–20 Jesus identifies the kinds of things that come from within which defile a person. Each of these can be related to one or more of the Ten Commandments. A Gentile Christian could and, I maintain, was expected to live by them. So, here is a distinction between two views of obedience to the Law.

One stems from Jesus, fixed more on the Ten Commandments. The other by the Pharisees, the Ten plus a host of other ceremonial regulations. Like other rabbis, Jesus discusses the essence of the law, but his combination of Deuteronomy and Leviticus is most famous: love of God and love of neighbor as oneself (Matt 22:37–40). "On these two commandments hang all of the law and the prophets" (Matt 22:40). At once, Jesus puts obedience to the Law in the reach of everyone and universalizes it so that none of us can flee its demand.

But how is this not a demand beyond the reach of ordinary people? Even people like us today?

The Sermon Begins with Beatitudes

"Makarios" is the Greek word for "blessed." Jesus begins the Sermon on the Mount with nine blessings. Just before, he had been going throughout Galilee, "proclaiming the good news of the kingdom." The crowds followed him from everywhere: "Galilee, the Decapolis, Jerusalem, Judea, and from beyond the Jordan" (Matt 4: 25). I believe that Matthew's intent is not to say that this is a diverse crowd geographically. Rather, everyone was drawn to this message of good news and the signs of the kingdom, performed from a heart of compassion.

It is no accident that he begins by blessing the people. Who were these people? Perhaps surprising from Rabbi Hillel, "There is no uneducated [person] who fears sin. Not one of the people of the land is religious."[2] From the point of view of the Jerusalem priesthood and the most pious Pharisees and scribes, ordinary folk, the people of the land, were not model Jews.

Yet, Jesus begins by blessing them. "Blessed are the poor in spirit, for theirs is the kingdom of heaven" (Matt 5:3). Allison and Davies in their

---

2. Bultmann, *Jesus and the Word*, 64.

extensive work on Matthew argue "that the Beatitudes are first of all blessings, not requirements. By opening the Sermon on the Mount they place it within the context of grace, and their function is very similar to the function of 4:23–5:२; just as healing comes before imperative, so does blessing come before demand. The precedence of grace could not be plainer. The hard commands of Matthew 5–7 presuppose God's mercy and prior saving activity."[3]

Grace has at least two meanings. One is forgiveness for sins confessed. Prior to that, grace is acceptance of people who are sinners. We might think of it this way: Before wondering whether or not God will forgive us of whatever troubles the conscience, is God on our side?

To imagine a deity of some kind is not to know what that deity's nature or attitude is. Is this god or goddess indifferent to humankind, off in a world to themselves? Do the gods even care what happens to us? Is there a sadistic side to the divine nature whereby god is out to get us? And if, as in Hinduism, there may be 33 million faces of deity (I always wondered who had actually counted them), which face is toward us on any given day?

Arguably the greatest rhetorical question in the Bible is that by the Apostle Paul in Rom 8:31, "If God is for us, who is against us?" "He who did not withhold his own Son, but gave him up for all of us, will he not with him also give us everything else?" (Rom. 8:32). Merely to speak of gods, goddesses, deities is not to say much. Who is God? Paul says, "God is for us" and ultimately self-giving.

Matthew says that Jesus is God with Us. To people who may have been marginalized by their society, not to mention Gentiles listening in, is God with us or for us? And how do we know?

Once I was with a family on a clear, cold winter's day at a cemetery on Long Island. I got out of the hearse and went to the grave site to test the footing. I could see snow on the hedge rows as the rest of the car procession made their way. From the snow and ice on the ground, there was a sloppy mixture near where the coffin was to be placed.

I didn't know this family, but as they stepped from their automobiles, I sensed how tentative they were. Not only because of slippery footing, but there seemed to be a reluctance to gather, either to one another or the grave. I asked them to move closer because a chill wind swept through the cemetery, and I wanted them to hear.

So, I began that day with the words, "If God is for us, who can be against us?" I paused. There was silence at the grave, only the wind whistling

---

3. Davies and Allison, *Critical and Exegetical Commentary*, Vol. 1, 439–440.

around. I said it again in case the words had been carried away. "If God is for us, who can be against us?"

Whether in Matthew's day or ours, footing is slippery at the grave. Who were these people Jesus addressed? We cannot know for sure, but they were in need of his words. "Blessed are the poor in spirit, for theirs is the kingdom of heaven." By God's grace, a new identity was on offer.

"Do not say, 'we have Abraham as our ancestor,'" said John the Baptist earlier in Matthew. A people of God are not made by their ancestry or claims to racial purity. They are made by God's covenant with them at the holy mountain. They are made by God in the person of the one speaking on a new mountain in Galilee.

Hope and Grapple

Let me collect several thoughts about traveling with Matthew. The Gospel tells a story of Jesus of Nazareth. The evangelist has drawn upon sources to include Jesus' deeds and sayings, his death, burial, and resurrection. But the author's purpose was never to write some kind of modern biography from which scholars could reconstruct exactly who Jesus was aside from the perspective of faith.

Rather, Matthew forwards the message of Jesus Christ, Emmanuel, God with Us for a community of believers later in the first century (about 80–95 CE). I maintain that Matthew has done in essence what modern preachers and theologians do. That is, receive words from the sacred past and apply them to contemporary situations.

Since Matthew, of the four Gospels, is most concerned with retrieving the story of Israel and relating it to the person and work of Jesus of Nazareth, we have a powerful example of using a great narrative to shape a message for a certain audience. How the evangelist does that is what energizes these pages.

But to develop that question, we must ask, how does Jesus embody the theme of God with Us by what he does and says? On the mountain of the Sermon on the Mount, he begins with blessings. On his lips, these express divine favor for the assembled people. God's grace is the first word event, we might say, as the crowd gathers on some mountain in Galilee.

Which mountain is less important for Matthew, I am arguing, than to understand it as a mountain like the one where God and Moses met. There is no thunder and lightning here, but as the Sermon concludes, an awesome authority attaches to Jesus' words.

Gracious words are not spoken indiscriminately. They are targeted to specific situations of need. As to the gathered people, they had not traveled an exodus path through the sea. We have no data on the crowd that day. But as any number of scholars have observed, Matthew gives us a clue by telling us Jesus' chosen residence for his ministry and referencing Isaiah (Matt 4:14–15).

"Jesus left Nazareth and made his home in Capernaum by the sea, in the territory of Zebulun and Naphtali, so that what had been spoken through the prophet Isaiah might be fulfilled: 'Land of Zebulun, land of Naphtali, on the road by the sea, across the Jordan, Galilee of the Gentiles—the people who sat in darkness have seen a great light, and for those who sat in the region and shadow of death, light has dawned" (Matt 4:13–16).

Galilee in those days was a mix of Jew and Gentile. Sepphoris, about ten miles from the sea, and four from Nazareth, was the largest city, and to this day, ruins show that it was a cosmopolitan place. On the other side of the Sea, the Decapolis, or "ten cities," was a region conquered by Alexander the Great and gifted to his generals for them to settle there. Which is to say, Galilee was different from Jerusalem and Judea to the south. It was a greater mix of peoples. It was a logical place from which "hope for the Gentiles" might spring as voiced by a prophet who took the vision of Isaiah to heart.

I suggest that it is no accident that Matthew gives us the diversity of the crowd which followed Jesus up the mountain, "from Galilee, the Decapolis, Jerusalem, Judea, and from beyond the Jordan" (Matt 4:25). Yes, people from everywhere were following Jesus. That is what Matthew is saying, but he is also showing us the mix that the quote from Isaiah and Jesus' residence in Capernaum indicate.

Which brings me to the point that Matthew cleverly wraps the message around Jesus while giving it direction and purpose. The more I travel with Matthew, the more this assessment by Raymond Brown seems true:

"Although the evangelist did draw on previously existing bodies of written and oral material, he did not produce a collection of glued-together sources. Working with a developed Christology, ecclesiology, and eschatology, he produced a highly effective narrative about Jesus that smoothly blended together what he received. That narrative won important parts of the ancient world to faith in Christ. It may be academically useful to detect the sources he employed, but to concentrate on the compositional background and miss the impact of the final product is to miss the beauty of the forest while counting the trees."[4]

---

4. Brown, *Introduction*, 208.

Not only in Matthew's Galilean flavoring of the crowds and Jesus' ministry, but in other ways we shall consider, this Gospel offers a coherent sense of who Jesus was and is. From blessings that express God's favor for the people, let us turn to what some sense as Matthew's more legalistic Jesus. Is that a fair reading?

CHAPTER EIGHT

God's Grace and Demand and Our Confusion

I BEGIN WITH A Hope and Grapple that has troubled me for most of my adult life. After the Beatitudes and the salt and light passages, Jesus says in the Sermon, "Do not think that I have come to abolish the law or the prophets but to fulfill. For truly I tell you, until heaven and earth pass away, not one letter, not one stroke of a letter, will pass from the law until all is accomplished. Therefore, whoever breaks one of the least of these commandments, and teaches others to do the same, will be called least in the kingdom of heaven; but whoever does them and teaches them will be called great in the kingdom of heaven. For I tell you, unless your righteousness exceeds that of the scribes and Pharisees, you will never enter the kingdom of heaven" (Matt 5: 17–20).

Jesus continues with teachings about anger, adultery, divorce, oaths, retaliation and love for enemies, showing how much better his followers should behave. Then he concludes by saying, "you shall be perfect as your father in heaven is perfect" (Matt 5:48).

Having been raised with a bent toward moral perfection, to hear that I or anyone should be perfect like God is a tough pill to swallow. Though I can blame my religious upbringing for an anemic theology of grace, I cannot blame them for my psychological make-up, which is attack dog enough.

When I say "moral perfection," I mean preoccupation with bettering oneself in accordance with God's will. At the same time, I am accompanied with a sense that I can never do enough and that failure lurks nearby. There are those who may be able to pursue a path of bettering themselves while maintaining emotional stability and charity toward themselves and others. But I am not one.

I bear some distant kinship with John Bunyan as William James described his condition: "He was a typical case of the psychopathic temperament, sensitive of conscience to a diseased degree, beset by doubts, fears and insistent ideas, and a victim of verbal automatisms, both motor and sensory. These were usually texts of Scripture which, sometimes damnatory and sometimes favorable, would come in a half-hallucinatory form as if they were voices, and fasten on his mind and buffet it between them like a shuttlecock. Added to this were a fearful melancholy, self-contempt and despair."[1]

Though Bunyan found relief in a profound experience of God, his struggle or condition, as James called it, is the extreme of what I and numerous others know well. And even though I know and trust God's grace, the harpies of my mind can still sink their claws in me.

Practically this means not only an occasional sense of worthlessness, but a tendency to hear in the oughts of the Bible or elsewhere a resounding overtone of condemnation. I can also suffer an attack when reading a piece of theology about God's wrath toward sin, or in church when a prayer of confession strikes me as oppressively lugubrious.

With such background noise at work, religious language can be distorted to sound as if God is playing a game of "gotcha." Perhaps needless to say, Lent has not been my favorite liturgical season.

Yes, I do know that the cross comes before the resurrection, and I have been reminded. To struggle with something well is not to ignore it but to clarify the nature of the struggle. To that goal, how do those of us with Lenten personalities cope with "remember that you are dust, and to dust you shall return"?

There are truly many facets to what I am describing, and those of us with some version of the attack dog find ourselves on a continuum as James also noted. Some of us have a "morbid mind" of a functional/ordinary sort while others, like Bunyan, range to the pathological. Personally, I thank God that Lent is but a season, and that my moods, like weather fronts, do pass through and clear. Personality types differ, but I have learned that there are enough of us who do not live on the sunny side of the street to take time with how we hear Jesus' words.

---

1. James, *Varieties of Religious Experience*, 132.

Blessed Are the Poor in Spirit to Be Ye Perfect

In a well-known essay, "The Apostle Paul and the Introspective Conscience of the West," the New Testament theologian Krister Stendahl argues that too much has been made of Paul's burden of conscience. Viewed as the psychological factor in his conversion, Paul feels a great weight of guilt, and he is relieved of it by his encounter with Christ. In brief, Stendahl says that the evidence in Paul's actual writings for such a tortured conscience is not there. Rather, before and after his conversion, his conscience is "robust."[2]

Stendahl's view is that we in the West have read Augustine and Luther back into Paul. Certainly the latter two conversions each evidence a stricken conscience. They both found a kindred spirit in Paul, and voila, Paul's conscience was stricken as well.

I do not want to enter that discussion except to grant Stendahl the point that we in the modern West do read the Scriptures through the lens of our particular psychological and cultural struggles. Were the biblical writers entirely free of any burden of scruples? I doubt it. But caution is necessary in not fashioning them in all ways like ourselves.

Hopefully such caution frees us to read the Sermon on the Mount with different eyes. For example, we have already wondered about Jesus' audience. It was not, by and large, the priests and Pharisees of Judea In fact, the ordinary, Jewish folk of Galilee were considered by some not model Jews.

From the point of view of the Pharisees and priests, they did not keep the law. We must keep in mind that Ezra and Nehemiah implemented a reordering of Jewish life after the exiles returned from Babylonian captivity. Believing that the deportation was God's punishment for Judah's idolatry as the prophets had said, they set about to purify themselves in such a way that the people would never suffer such divine displeasure again.

This new way became a strict racial, religious, and ritual purity. No doubt, it was a way of preserving Jewish identity through troubled times, as Gerd Theissen has observed.[3] But by the days of Jesus, the Pharisees, in another renewal movement, begun during the restoration of the Maccabees, had picked up the old separatist themes of racial, religious and ritual purity.

The New Testament scholar Marcus Borg has called this "the politics of holiness" or "the holiness code." Drawing on the work of other scholars like W.D. Davies, Joachim Jeremias, Jacob Neusner, Gerd Theissen, and his

---

2. Stendahl, *Harvard Theological Review*, 199–215.
3. Theissen, *Early Palestinian Christianity*, 77.

own research (*Conflict, Holiness and Politics in the Teaching of Jesus*), Borg has written:

"The politics of holiness was a continuation in intensified form of a cultural dynamic that had emerged in Judaism after the exile. It was expressed most succinctly in the 'holiness code' whose central words affirmed, 'You shall be holy, as I the Lord your God am holy' . . . To be holy meant to be separate from everything that would defile holiness."[4]

Continuing with Borg, "From the Pharisaic point of view, the most offensive of the nonobservant were said to have lost all civil and religious rights; they were deprived of the right to sit on local councils and lost their place as children of Abraham in the life of the age to come. They became 'as Gentiles.'

"The major vehicle of social and religious ostracism was the refusal of table fellowship. To share a meal with a person was an expression of acceptance; to refuse to share a meal symbolized disapproval and rejection. Accordingly, Pharisees would not share a meal with the nonobservant."[5]

Borg draws an analogy from Hindu culture in illustrating the outcast nature of some persons in Israel of that day. He is careful to say that for social and religious outcasts in Jesus' day, theirs was not a status that was hereditary as was that in Hindu mythology and practice. But the taint of being outcast in one's own land is a psychology we should not overlook.

In India years ago, I had occasion to talk with James Massey, a delightful man and *dahlit* theologian. "*Dahlit*" is the term for outcastes in India. Though people may now be doctors and lawyers, the untouchable nature of their upbringing and history still resonates in their sense of identity.

For this reason, Dr. Massey told me that original sin was not a Christian doctrine that he taught in India. In its Augustinian version of sin as carnally-generated to and through all humanity from Adam and Eve (Augustine should not be judged by this alone), it bears too much resemblance to the cultural view of *dahlit* status, which, in the caste system, is essentially status-less. Some make the mistake of thinking that *dahlits* are the bottom rung of the caste system, but they are not even on the ladder. This is another example of how cultural myths, attitudes, and prejudices can distort our reading of Scripture and theology.

We cannot know the self-identity of the people who first heard Jesus' Sermon on the Mount, but could this be one reason that Jesus was throughout the Beatitudes reminding them of God's favor? In other words, the people who were "not my people" are "now my people," to quote the

---

4. Borg, *Jesus a New Vision*, 86.
5. Borg, *Jesus a New Vision*, 89.

prophet Hosea (Hosea 1:8–9; 2:23; 1 Peter 2:9–10). And to quote another prophet, was he saying to them, "I will put my law within them, and I will write it on their hearts; and I will be their God, and they shall be my people" (Jeremiah 31:33)?

In point of fact, Jesus in the Sermon is not laying a burden on the people, but rather, he is putting obedience to the Law within their reach. In effect, he is saying, "It is not only the priests and Pharisees who can obey the Law and be God's people, but you can too." This was a new identity for people who may have seen themselves as outsiders to the Jerusalem cult of sacrifice, or, at least, not as worthy.

"Be perfect, therefore, as your heavenly Father is perfect" may not be accenting what God expects of us, that is, some kind of flawless behavior. Rather, Jesus may be saying that God alone is the standard for us all, not the scribes and Pharisees.

I suggest further that Jesus is not saying that you and I ought to be as God. Rather, we ought to stand as tall as God intends us to stand. Put more in modern jargon, Jesus is calling us to stand before God to the true height of our humanity. I realize that sounds a bit like the Army slogan, "Be all you can be," but the Army aside, ours is not some measure of perfection by either the Pharisees or our neighbors. It is Christ's call that we be what God intends that we be; that is, you and I.

Ultimately, I am judged by God according to the capacities of the person God made me. The same is true of my neighbor. And as the psalmist said, "God knows how we were made; God remembers that we are dust" (Ps. 103:14). No one else is our judge and redeemer. God alone on the height raises us to our full stature.

Against the backdrop of viewing Jesus in the midst of some Jewish ethic of legalism, Rudolph Bultmann once observed, "As an ethic of obedience the Jewish morality was not designed from the human standpoint; that is, its purpose is not the realization of an ideal [human being] or humanity. It is definitely opposed to all humanistic ethics, for in it not [human beings] but only the glory of God is important."[6]

In this respect, any number of Jews today could be helpful to Christians when we tie ourselves in emotional knots as to who we should be and what we should do. That God is perfect does not mean that we should live without failure or sin. Rather, it means that ultimately we live before God who is both gracious and demanding but with respect to who each one of us is, not how we compare ourselves to others.

---

6. Bultmann, *Jesus and the Word*, 55.

A Bit More Grappling

The Greek word "teleios" may be translated "complete," "perfect," or "mature." The New Testament scholar and textual expert Bruce M. Metzger has noted that the root of "teleios" is "tel," meaning "end," from which a family of words derives. Thus, the adjective "teleios" signifies that which is "brought to its appropriate end."[7]

Though I believe the sense of words must be read from a context of usage, the way that the root of a word family develops is relevant. From two directions, context and word study, "Be perfect as your father in heaven is perfect" speaks to me, not of moral perfection, as if humans are to be behaviorally sinless like God. Rather, we are to be drawn into our own completeness and maturity by rising to our full height before God.

This rescues us from a granular reading of the Gospels and getting lost in all the ways we cannot "be perfect" in that unique and impossible sense for us of being without sin. It helps to keep our eyes on the whole of who we are before God and the fact that God favors us to stand tall.

With the strict demands in Matthew and the other Gospels, we may be deeply puzzled, like the disciples who asked Jesus, "Then who can be saved?" (Matt 19:26). If that young, rich, and righteous man had to turn away, what hope is there for us who have not been so blessed? Riches were, for many in that day, a sign of special blessing. For this reason, Jesus' saying, "it will be harder for the [especially blessed] to enter the kingdom than for a camel to go throw the eye of a needle," was met with a strong reaction. "Then who can be saved?"

Jesus then arrests their vision fixed on themselves and refocuses it on God. "With humans, this is not possible, but with God, all things are possible" (Matt 19:26). Following the Savior, we can trip over hurdles of our own construction. A sustained self-focus can see quitting the journey as its only option to secure release from a rigidly self-critical mind, foisting upon itself the burden of hopelessness.

No one knows better than Jesus that such a distorted viewpoint can train its eyes on others. It takes their measure solely to find specks in their eyes or cracks in their moral stature (Matt 7:1–5). But traveling with Matthew, we need keep our eyes on the God who is for us, and what God does with us, and not stumble on the stones of what we cannot do and be. This is the wide and life-giving vision of God and the good news.

---

7. Metzger, *Lexical Aids*, 41.

A Note on the Order and Nature of Obedience

Years ago, I heard a lecture by Father Henri Nouwen, a wonderful pastoral theologian. He said that the word "obedience" derives from Latin, meaning "to hear."

Nouwen told us about disobedient monks who left the confessional where they were absolved from their sins, but did not truly hear (receive) the words of forgiveness. Were we merely to pass over or pass by the Beatitudes to Jesus' teaching about a better righteousness, we would be disobedient. God's law is prefaced by grace.

"Then God spoke all these words: 'I am the Lord your God, who brought you out of the land of Egypt, out of the house of slavery'" (Exod 20:1–2). Before the Ten Commandments, God reminds Israel of their redemption from bondage. It is this redeeming God who gives the law. It is not an "out-to-getcha god."

Similarly the better righteousness that Jesus puts in the reach of the crowd in Galilee proceeds from the mouth of God with Us, the God of the Beatitudes. To miss the preface in Exodus 20 or the Beatitudes in Matthew 5 is to be disobedient according to Nouwen's word study.

Over the years there were four clergy that met annually. We were Anglican, Disciples, Presbyterian, and Roman Catholic. Within that cluster of friends was grace—"Where two or three are gathered in my name" (Matt 18:20). I could hear most anything they said to me and take it to heart because I knew they cared for me.

Knowing that God is profoundly for us is the basis of our hearing the call to stand tall. The direction from grace to law is extremely important. God first redeemed us. God first is with us. God embraces us and will not let go. Consequently, God addresses us to live in a relationship of love toward God, neighbor, and inwardly toward ourselves (Matt 22).

Maintaining the priority of God in the moral life is what Bultmann meant when he said that "Jewish morality is an ethic of obedience" oriented toward the glory of God. It is not a "humanistic ethic."[8] As Jews and Christians, people of the book, we are not about displaying heroic virtue, or rendering gold-medal performances on the uneven bar. "And none, O Lord, have perfect rest, for none are wholly free from sin; And they who fain would serve Thee best are conscious most of wrong within."[9] Put another way, we can trip over our own feet and lose sight of the God who extends a hand to save us.

---

8. Bultmann, *Jesus and the Word*, 55.
9. Twells, "At Even When the Sun Was Set."

When I have gotten in my own way, this passage from Samuel Johnson's "Rasselas" has been helpful. What follows are the words of the wise Imlac who counsels Rasselas, the Prince of Abysinnia. Pekuah is a delightful friend of Rasselas' sister, the princess.

"Open your heart to the influence of the light, which, from time to time, breaks in upon you: when scruples importune you which you in your more lucid moments know to be vain, do not stand to parley, but fly to business or Pekuah, and keep this thought always prevalent, that you are only one atom of the mass of humanity, and have neither such virtue nor vice that you should be singled out for supernatural favors or afflictions."[10]

Trusting that God's grace upholds us, we may rest within God's care that frees us from the presumption that neither our sins nor afflictions loom large in the scope of all things. Even so, I have encountered a person or two who seemed to take pride in how great their sins or sufferings had been. But standing tall on a dossier of how bad life has been for us is a risky perch. Rather, we rise daily to God's mercies, which are enough to sustain us to be the persons we need to be. If the day does not go well, we rise again tomorrow.

At this point, I nod to the theologian Dietrich Bonhoeffer, who turned to Matthew and the other Gospels for reflections on the meaning of discipleship, not first to Paul and justification by grace through faith. Bonhoeffer felt that the concept of grace had been overused particularly in a world where too many in the name of Christ were going along with Hitler when opposition was necessary. "Cheap grace," he famously called it.[11]

I understand what he meant and greatly respect his mind and his heart and his ultimate witness. But also reading Matthew, I hold to the view that grace is how we begin to answer God's call. And no matter how far we may go or need to go, to set out on our own is like Peter stepping out on the water to Jesus but sinking in his fear of the waves.

Grace is the ground on which we stand to follow Christ. "The Way," he called it in John's Gospel (John 14:6). It is not cheap except if we refuse to put our full weight on it, not realizing how much we are in need of it. No doubt, what Christ calls us to do and be in any given moment of life may be hard, the fears we must face, the loneliness we must abide, the sheer load we must carry.

Faith takes grace by the hand to know that God is most profoundly with Us in the most tangled web of confusion and wrong. Just as God was with Israel and the disciples in their greatest confusion and wrong, the one

---

10. Johnson, *Selected Writings*, 250.
11. Bonhoeffer, *Cost of Discipleship*, 45.

obscured by the cross on which he hangs is yet God in the midst of human sin and suffering. Grace is never some shallow permission we allow ourselves to abandon the task or to run away. It is the call of Jesus that we come before God on the height. In God's presence we are drawn up to our full height and learn therein that the one who demands is also gracious. The gracious one will not leave us alone.

In our saying "yes" to the call of Christ, we are responding to a hand beyond our strength, extended to us even when we sink and must be shouldered back to the boat. Particularly when we fall and must crawl back, we learn that God's mercies are new every morning

CHAPTER NINE

The Joy of the Kingdom

HAVING GIVEN A NOD to Dietrich Bonhoeffer, I now give more than a nod. His dismissal of "cheap grace" for "costly grace" has a context we cannot ignore. Following Christ always occurs in a context of what swirls around us and within. By all accounts, Bonhoeffer was someone who bore the weight of serious times without being paralyzed by melancholy. This is not to say that he never felt lost in dark moods nor suffer piercing sadness. Yet, as a friend, he was known for his playfulness. As a fellow prisoner, for his calm and encouragement.

In this chapter, we'll focus more on the context within or the kingdom that has come near. In chapter 10, the context that swirled about Jesus.

Referencing Matthew, Bonhoeffer wrote in *The Cost of Discipleship*, "Costly grace is the gospel which must be sought again and again, the gift which must be asked for, the door at which a [person] must knock.

"Such grace is costly because it calls us to follow, and it is grace because it calls us to follow Jesus Christ. It is costly because it costs [a person's] life, and it is grace because it gives a [person] the only true life."[1]

Going the way of the cross was hard for Jesus' disciples. Three times in Matthew, Mark, and Luke, Jesus tells them about his suffering death to come in Jerusalem. In Matthew 16, Peter famously says, "God forbid, Lord; this will not be the way for you" (Matt 16:22). But Jesus says to him, "get behind me, Satan."

One might expect that Jesus would be filled with melancholy since he was so aware of his end. I must say here that I believe that Jesus had an extraordinary prescience about things to come. Even if the later church may

---

1. Bonhoeffer, *Cost of Discipleship*, 47.

have exaggerated what Jesus actually knew in his lifetime, there is no reason to believe that he could not perceive what was coming. Dr. King certainly read the signs of what would be his end. Jesus no less so.

So, why was his mind not constantly weighed down with sorrow? It was in Gethsemane (Matt 26), we are told, and on the cross (Matt 27). But those were situations in which he was suffering extensively, both emotionally and physically. And yet, on the journey itself, Jesus proclaims the kingdom and the joy of it.

"The kingdom of heaven is like a treasure hidden in a field which a man found and hid. And out of great joy he went and sold all that he had and bought that field" (Matt 13:44).

"Again the kingdom of heaven is like a gem merchant, seeking an exquisite pearl. And finding one of great value, departing, he sold all he had and bought it" (Matt 13:45–46).

At the beginning of Jesus' ministry, he proclaimed, "Repent for the kingdom of heaven is near" (Matt 4:17). Mark says, "Repent and believe in the good news" (Mark 1:15). Jesus' joyful proclamation in Matthew does not use the word "joy" or "good" at this point but instead references Isaiah: "Those who sat in the region and shadow of death, on them light has dawned" (Matt 4:16).

Then after calling the fisherfolk, and "going about the whole of Galilee, teaching in their synagogues and proclaiming the good news of the kingdom, he healed all they brought to him" (Matt 4:18–22; 23–25). It was this crowd that followed him up the mountain and on whom he pronounced the blessings at the beginning of the sermon. Good news, light dawning, healing and divine favor, these are the treasure of joy worth selling all one has to find.

Though the way gets hard and the sun does not shine at the end, the joy of this journey is not snuffed out. The women, after encountering the angel with the message, "He is risen from the dead," went as they were instructed to tell the male disciples. Matthew adds, "They departed the tomb quickly with fear and great joy" (Matt 28:8). John Donne comments, "The women, angels of the resurrection, went from the sepulchre with fear and joy; they ran, says the text, and they ran upon those two legs, fear and joy; and both was the right leg; they joy in thee, O Lord, that fear thee, and fear thee only, who feel this joy in thee. Nay, thy fear, and thy love are inseparable."[2]

In Matthew 28, the word translated "fear," "phobos," could easily include the emotion of "awe." For their spines must have tingled in the grip of life, not only beyond death, but beyond any sense of life they had ever

---

2. Donne, *Devotions*, 40.

known. Heading straightway into the path of Jesus, they heard him say, "Be of good cheer," the verb form of "joy." This is a way of joy.

Blessings We Must Seek

In the quote above, Bonhoeffer refers to the "ask, seek, knock" passage of Matthew 7: "For everyone who asks, receives, and everyone who seeks, shall find, and for everyone who knocks, it shall be opened" (Matt 7:8). What follows is a parable of God's bounty: "If we who are wicked [meaning ordinary humans] know how to give good things to our children when they ask, how much more will your father in heaven give good things to those who ask him" (Matt 7:11).

Bonhoeffer picks up the sense of the text in saying, "Costly grace is the gospel which must be sought again and again, the gift which must be asked for, the door at which [a person] must knock."[3] It is as if Jesus is saying, "We cannot know, perhaps, even imagine, how gracious God is unless we practice opening ourselves to receive what God gladly gives."

In this context in the Sermon on the Mount, Jesus follows with the parable about the straight gate and the narrow way. "The gate is straight and the way is narrow that leads to life, and few there are that find it" (Matt 7:14). The Greek words "stenos" and "thlibo," translated "straight" and "narrow," both have the sense of something hard to pass through.

On the surface, "ask, seek, knock" and "the straight and narrow" seem to contradict one another. One is about God's generosity, grace. The other about a way that leads to destruction which many find, and the few who make it to life.

We may dislike the sound of the narrow way and opt for a more generous God. Or, we may feel justified in going that more difficult path. This might entail ignoring one or the other.

But I'll introduce here a view that trying to reconcile or do away with apparent contradictions is searching for a logic tighter than Jesus. Rather, traveling with Matthew, the gracious God is always prior to our response, coming before us with hand extended to our lesser obedience. It is an emphasis which we must keep before us because many things distract us. And much that happens oppresses us, leading to a despairing vision that can lose its way.

It is a fact that Jesus' words do sometimes resound with a prophet's warning. "To the hard of hearing, you shout, and for the almost-blind, you

---

3 Bonhoeffer, *Cost of Discipleship*, 47.

draw large and startling figures."[4] In this way of crafting the word of God, the prophet was always calling Israel back. And Jesus was both full of grace and passionate warning. We need not make a choice between them.

Hope and Grapple: Fleeing Gloom

Years ago I was fascinated by the book *Jesus of Nazareth* by the New Testament theologian Gunther Bornkamm. When my wife and I and another couple thought some prayerful discussion of religious themes would benefit us, I recommended we read Bornkamm together. But to my disappointment and hurt feelings, as I recall, they did not take to it.

Why I did and they did not is not a mystery. I have been nurtured in faith by readings which require a certain kind of mind. My wife calls me "musty" though she actually appreciates my preaching, which has drawn upon the cobwebs and dust.

Truth be told, I have read *Jesus of Nazareth* over and over, by which I mean maybe five times over the course of my life. Certain passages I have gone to more frequently.

It should come as no surprise that a particular favorite is a section entitled "Joyful Living." I quote in full the pertinent passage.

"Again and again in the Gospels the deep gloom which hangs over the righteousness of the 'good' becomes apparent; in the grumbling of the Pharisees and scribes over Jesus' eating with sinners; in the indignation with which they hear the words of forgiveness that he speaks to the sick of palsy (Mark 2:6f.); in the anger they show when they call him 'a glutton and drunkard' (Matt 11:19); in the wrath aroused in them by the cries of joy that greet Jesus as he rides into Jerusalem (Matt 21:15f.). This joylessness can be heard in the prayer of thanks offered up by the Pharisee as he sets out all his pious words before God as in a shop-window (Luke 18:9ff.), and in his righteousness profits by the guilt of others. It is heard in the parable of the prodigal son, in the words addressed to the father by the elder son, when he remains outside and refuses to take part in the feast: 'You never gave me a kid, that I might make merry with my friends' (Luke 15:29): and again in the complaint of the first laborers to be hired in the parable of the laborers in the vineyards (Matt 20: 1ff.), that those who were hired last receive the same reward from their master. But this is the very thing which decides who will finally be lost, who in the end are the first and who the last. 'Or do you begrudge my generosity?' is the lord's last word to the grumblers in the parable of the laborers. 'It was fitting to make merry and be glad; for this your

---

4. O'Connor, *Mystery and Manners*, 34.

brother was dead, and is alive; he was lost and is found,' were the last words of the father to the elder brother. The joy is the joy of the deliverance from death. It is a matter of nothing less than this. For this reason the last words in both parables, far from sounding a note of reproach and fault-finding, have a note of questioning and of urgent persuasion. What becomes of the prodigal son, we know; but what will become of the elder brother?"[5]

I have not read another author who has so closely read the Gospels and picks up this theme so wonderfully. Bornkamm does not import joy and grumbling to the text. They are clearly there, but it took a keen interpreter to open my eyes to see it.

And how I need it. As the poet George Herbert once wrote:

> Lord mend or rather make us: one creation
> Will not suffice our turn:
> Except Thou make us daily, we shall spurn
> Our own salvation.[6]

Herbert was well aware by his own temperament and/or his insight into human nature that our hearts and minds require constant tending and shaping by the gospel.

While on Long Island, I said more than once in sermons that "complaint is the conversational default of New Yorkers." At that time I identified myself as a New Yorker and in this way I still do. In fairness, I noted that we often do not mean anything by our complaints about the weather, the traffic, politicians, prices in the grocery store, taxes, and the like. It is simply the way we make conversation and connect with one another.

But, there is a time to turn off the complaint default, lest unknowingly it eats away our spirits. We of the church need that reminder. If we like our congregations and parishes we should say so. If we are counting our blessings, we should give thanks. If we have truly been touched by God's grace and healing hand, we should seek a time and a place to help others bear their burdens.

There was a joy that came through in Jesus' message and abided in him. Even on a path to his death, he took joy. And to be factual, not only existential, "None of us is getting out of here alive," says my wise wife. We are all on a path through death to life. The impassioned plea of the gospel is that we stay alert and pay attention to the signs of the kingdom along the way. There is joy. So, "ask, seek, knock." Every day.

---

5. Bornkamm, *Jesus of Nazareth*, 85.
6. Herbert, *Country Parson and the Temple*, 250.

CHAPTER TEN

The Swirl of Life Around Jesus

OVER THE COURSE OF my life, I have imagined a future without any stress or sadness. When I talk with acquaintances who are still in the throes of active employment, I hear how wistful they are when I announce that I am retired. My hunch is that most of us, while coping with the challenges of a certain season, can become wistful about a beach, a book, and a cool drink or some such. But the truth is, each season ebbs and flows with wonder and worry. For that reason, "ask, seek, knock" do not represent a one-time conversion experience but spiritual actions or disciplines we need to take throughout the journey.

No doubt, some seasons of life and certain times are harder than others. Bonhoeffer believed that Hitler had stolen Germany from its heritage. In doing so, the Nazis had co-opted the Christian church. Therefore, it was incumbent upon Christians to live and clearly articulate their faith at a time when many were being called upon to give the Third Reich their complete loyalty or face death.

Bonhoeffer was hanged at the concentration camp at Flossenburg on April 9, 1945, just a few days before it was liberated by the Allied forces. His times put his life and theology in a framework for making radical choices. For him discipleship and grace, grace and discipleship, were about following Jesus to the cross. When others cheapen human existence as the Nazis did, following Jesus must show who God intends that we be.

I lift up the more recent and fairly well-known history of Bonhoeffer's years to draw an analogy with Jesus on his journey to Jerusalem. Bonhoeffer's theology came into sharp focus against the honing reality of Nazi Germany. What did Jesus face?

By reflecting on Jesus as God with Us, we might imagine him, "wandering" the hills of Galilee "lonely as a cloud" with heaven on his mind. No doubt, Matthew and the other gospels depict Jesus as self-possessed in his purpose. But the fact that he instructs the disciples three separate times about his end in Matthew, Mark, and Luke (Matt 16, 17, 20; Mark 8, 9, 10; Luke 9, 9, 18) is like an ominous cloud overshadowing this story. I suggest that this literary sky of the Gospels reflects events that were very much on the ground.

Gaps in Christian Knowledge

Reading the Gospels without much background, we can make a certain sense of it. Once after an elder had read the crucifixion story to her young son, he asked, almost tearfully, "But mom, where were the good guys?" Everything and everyone seemed, even to a child, aligned against Jesus as he found himself between a dark sky and his own people. The story as we first hear or read it has power to break through to us.

And yet, there are contours of this journey we can miss because we are unfamiliar with the territory. In confirmation class, I would ask about the maps of Palestine we had drawn, "How is it that Jericho is northeast of Jerusalem, but Jesus said, 'A man went down from Jerusalem to Jericho'?"

The answer is, of course, that Jericho is a steep drop in elevation from Jerusalem even though it lies to the northeast. This is a literal difference in the contour of the land that figures into the sense of the story. But there are contours of culture shaped by history, Scripture, and tradition. These too make up the landscape of the Gospels. We could view these in a variety of ways, but I choose the kaleidoscope of three Jewish attitudes toward the Roman occupation of Palestine.

Before turning that cylinder, we in the church may need to fill the gaps in our knowledge with a bit more Jewish history. The Bible in our hands jumps from Malachi to Matthew if we are not aware of those books in between called "apocryphal" or "deutero-canonical." Not every volume in this corpus carries equal weight, but 1 Maccabees offers an important history of a Jewish rebellion against domination by the Seleucid ruler known as Antiochus Epiphanes.

After a military campaign against Egypt, Antiochus went home to Syria by way of Jerusalem, where he entered the temple. First Maccabees says, "He went up against Israel and came to Jerusalem with a strong force. He arrogantly entered the sanctuary and took the golden altar, the lampstand for the light, and all its utensils. He took also the table for the bread of the

Presence . . . He shed much blood, and spoke with great arrogance. Israel mourned deeply in every community, rulers and elders groaned, young women and young men became faint, the beauty of the women faded" (1 Macc 1:20-26).

Two years later, Antiochus's forces returned when "they erected a desecrating sacrilege on the altar of burnt offering" in the temple. Three times Daniel makes reference to this desecration (Dan. 9:27; 11:31; 12:11). Matthew does the same (Matt 24:15), employing the language of Daniel which, though written as the product of a dream, signifies the actual desecration of Antiochus. Maccabees, of course, tells the story in straightforward prose narrative, not a visionary frame, as in Daniel.

Though Matthew uses Daniel differently to point forward to another time of desecration, Daniel, 1 Maccabees, and Matthew share the same memory of a terrible affront to Israel, Jerusalem, and the temple. It was this tragic occurrence of the desecrating sacrilege in 165 BCE that prompted Mattathias and his five sons to engage with Antiochus. Their military victories ushered in one hundred years of relative independence for the Jews (164 BCE to 63 BCE).

Though Mattathias's family name was the Hasmoneans, the Maccabees came to be used because Judas, one of Mattathias' sons, was known as "the Hammer" for his military exploits. Maccabees probably derives from "maqabi," transliteration of the Hebrew word for hammer. Toward the end of the Hasmonean dynasty, two rival Jewish rulers, John Hyrcanus II and Aristobulus II, engaged in a civil war for control of the land, people, Jerusalem, and the temple.

Pompey, the Roman general, stationed in Syria to the north, watched this fight from a distance. When it seemed to destabilize the region, he moved down with his forces. Laying siege to Jerusalem for several months, he eventually entered the city victorious and established the Roman occupation which was in place throughout Jesus' lifetime.

This history occupied the memories of those who populate the gospels. The Maccabean revolt and victory was celebrated by the feast of Hanukkah, mentioned as the Feast of Dedication in John's Gospel (John 10:22). "At that time the Festival of Dedication took place in Jerusalem. It was winter, and Jesus was walking in the temple, in the portico of Solomon." Dedication commemorated the purification of the temple in 164 BCE after its desecration by Antiochus' forces in 167 and 165 BCE, which led to the rebellion.

As we move into the Gospels, particularly traveling with Matthew, there are several takeaways from the history I have briefly sketched. One is the fact that less than two hundred years before Jesus and his contemporaries, the Jews had achieved a lasting victory from an oppressive foreign power.

Two, as 1 Maccabees makes clear, this was perceived as a victory over the Gentiles. Antiochus had attacked the Jews and desecrated just about every aspect of their identity. More than Jewish pride, Jewish piety (identity) was at stake. Circumcision, keeping Sabbath, kosher tables, thus devoting themselves to the Torah, were hallmarks of faithfulness to the God of the covenant.

Three, though a number of Jews at that time interacted freely with Gentiles, when their very existence was under attack, protecting their identity took on greater importance. Christians have tended to portray the marks of Judaism as steps taken to earn their salvation, but this view misses the point. In contexts where a people is threatened, the need for preservation surfaces in questions about belonging and distinction. N.T. Wright puts it well: "Those on the frontier get into trouble if they do not keep the boundary fences in good repair."[1]

Four, during the Hasmonean dynasty, the separatist sect known as the Pharisees came into being. Their modus vivendi was to maintain devotion to God and the covenant. The signs and symbols of this covenant, circumcision, Sabbath, ritual purity, temple, land, people, all derived from the Torah. The Pharisees were about stricter observance. This meant doubling down on the marks of identity which, in their view, increased a sense of belonging and kept Jews from assimilation. It was not only attacks from Gentiles that concerned them but the compromising tendencies of the Hasmonean rulers themselves.

Five, as numerous biblical scholars have observed, however we interpret separation of church and state in modern America and other nations, we cannot legitimately read that into either the Hebrew or Christian Scriptures. Signs and symbols of the covenant were signs and symbols of the people whom God had chosen. The political power they attained, lost, and/or aspired to was part and parcel of an integrated sphere of secular and religious life, as we might say it. Not until the total destruction of Jerusalem and the temple in 135 CE did a form of Judaism instructed by the Rabbis lead to a more quietistic way of life because religious Jews (Jews of any leaning, for that matter) were no longer in control of the state. This was simply because the political entity that had been Israel was no more, and would not be again until modern times.

---

1. Wright, *New Testament*, 168.

Six, we must draw an important conclusion from reading the relevant texts. Daniel (written at the time of the Maccabees), 1 Maccabees, and Matthew each share a similar history. They encompass events that were described both in prosaic narrative and apocalyptic imagery. Matthew, Mark, Luke, and Revelation in the New Testament employ apocalyptic symbols and images. Comparing Matthew, Mark, Daniel, and 1 Maccabees in their use of "the desecrating sacrilege," we can better see how both poetry and prose can refer to actual events of the time. None of this literature is unmoored from history, though it may direct attention to future acts of God. We must take care not to set the apocalyptic symbols and signs in the Bible on a false trajectory to refer to people and events far beyond the times in which they belong.

I feel that I must add a brief word, hopefully clarifying, about the concept "apocalyptic." It designates a literary genre of the Bible, employing images and symbols to indicate the end of an era. Actual events and persons are in reference, but veiled by the imagery. Larger-than-life, even grotesque figures represent the struggle between life and death. Conflict among nations couples with disturbing changes in earth, sea, and sky to portray colossal shifts in the times.

Such troubling forces issue the cry among God's people, "How long, O Lord?" How long will chaos and confusion reign and wreak unbearable suffering and anguish? In response, a divine/human figure symbolizes God's coming power and presence to bring judgment and salvation to bear on an evil hour.

The use of apocalyptic in the Bible is to give hope in the triumph of God through a dense moral and spiritual darkness. When life is shrouded by death, Matthew 24, for example, offers a literary landscape that addresses changing times and terrible suffering with exhortation to endure because the Son of Man is coming.

To understand Jesus in his times, it is necessary to have some grasp of the apocalyptic worldview and the other five factors of life and language that I have identified from his recent history. What dynamic did that history set in motion among Jesus and his contemporaries?

Turning the Kaleidoscope

As discussed above, there were three Jewish attitudes toward their Roman overlords. Another way of putting this might be to identify a variety of Jewish roles and sects of the period: priests, Sadducees, Pharisees, Essenes, and zealots, to mention the oft-identified players of biblical study. But some of these were more central to Jesus' story than others. And the Pharisees, for example, may have varied in their attitudes toward Rome and the Gentiles, taking up now one role and again another.

I choose, rather, a safer course than trying to define the various groups according to what they believed at any one time. Prevalent practices are better indicators. Like dust clouds stirred up by movement on the ground, there were three clusters of opinion Jews held toward their Roman occupiers. Jesus on his journey to Jerusalem had to negotiate his way among them.

As we turn the kaleidoscope to see one grouping, we find those who wanted to continue the work of the Maccabees; that is, to form militias to overthrow the occupiers with the sword. One example is a revolt in 6 CE by Judas the Galilean. It was stopped by Roman might and brutally suppressed by lining a road in Palestine with two thousand crosses. This was a terrible Roman signal to anyone else who might try such a thing. The cross itself was intended as that kind of deterrent.

Was Judas a zealot, someone defined by the cause of freedom from the Romans? Or, as N.T. Wright wonders, was Judas, as Josephus leaves room to imagine, a Pharisee or closely allied with them?[2] Recently (May 7–9, 2019) there was a scholar's conference convened in Rome to discuss "Jesus and the Pharisees." Were Pharisees about Torah observance or militia movements? Or, did they go along with the Romans just enough to secure a peaceful environment for their way of life? As I indicated, they may have leaned this way at one time and that at another.

Let us say, if I were of a mind to rally support for a rebellion against some powerful dictator, not to mention be part of one, I probably wouldn't placard my views down Main Street. In other words, my stance might be furtive, my views coded. Neither would be easy for a contemporary to detect, not to mention a historian.

Which leads us to persons who hid in caves and held clandestine meetings to oust the Romans, Pharisees or not. Jesus, according to Luke, may have been mistaken for a messiah of that kind, even by his own followers. "Lord, is this the time when you will restore the kingdom to Israel?" (Acts 1:6). We must remember that a messiah was thought to be a leader who would arise to free the people and establish a kingdom like that of David, the prototypical messiah.

By contrast, what we read in Matthew are strong words about peace. "Blessed are the peacemakers, for they will be called children of God" (Matt 5:9). "I say to you, do not resist an evildoer. But if anyone strikes you on the right cheek, turn the other also" (Matt 5:39). "Then Jesus said to him, 'Put

---

2. Wright, *New Testament*, 191.

your sword back in its place; for all who take the sword will perish by the sword'" (Matt 26:52). These familiar phrases stand out when we realize that ordinary people lived under the burden of Roman taxation and with the familiar sight of soldiers traveling their roads. Certainly ordinary Jews knew the story of the Maccabees which they celebrated at Hanukkah each wintertime.

Turning the kaleidoscope again, we see another configuration of Roman opposition. We might think of it as those, like some Pharisees, who doubled down on Jewish identity due to the cultural pressures to assimilate. We might not realize that there were sizeable, mostly Gentile, cities in Palestine. Sepphoris was only about four miles from Nazareth. Beth Shean but four miles from Mt. Gilboa in the central hill country where King Saul met his end. By strict Jewish standards, these cities were full of idols and immorality.

Caesar's image on the coinage brought to mind both idolatry and taxes. Jesus had to negotiate his way through a thicket of opposition when some Pharisees along with supporters of King Herod asked him, "Is it lawful to pay taxes to the emperor or not?" (Matt 22: 17).

Earlier in Matthew (chapter 9), Pharisees raised questions about Jesus eating with tax collectors and sinners. Tax collectors were Jews recruited by Romans to receive revenue from their own people. What was worse, they were allowed to keep some for themselves as an incentive.

Who were the sinners? We don't know for sure. Were they Jews who were not strictly observant? An example may have been Jewish merchants who were dependent on Gentiles for their livelihood. Then there were women thought to be as bad as prostitutes because they were publicly seen in the company of men, even some of Jesus' disciples (Matt 27:55–56). We don't know exactly who the sinners were, but Jesus, sitting at table with tax collectors and sinners, accrues to himself guilt by association. He is with the wrong crowd, the not-keeping-the-Torah-well-enough crowd.

In Matthew 15, Jesus offends the Pharisees and scribes by reversing the teaching and practice of washing hands and other purity rituals. He dares to say, "It is not what goes into the mouth that defiles a person, but it is what comes out . . . out of the heart come evil intentions, murder, adultery, fornication, theft, false witness, slander. These are what defile a person, but to eat with unwashed hands does not defile" (Matt 15: 11, 19).

In listing wrongs from the heart, Jesus basically refers to the Ten Commandments. Gentiles could observe these. And this may be the offense, that Jesus obscures the boundary between Jew and Gentile. His vision of the people of God differs from theirs. Throughout Matthew from the Gentile magi who follow the star to Jesus' commission to all the world, there is a wide vision of the people of God. As the light of the star itself suggests, this story is about Israel's role as "a light to the nations" (Isa 42:6).

One more turn of the kaleidoscope focuses on the Jewish leaders, particularly the chief priests, Sadducees, and some Pharisees, who made up the Sanhedrin in Jerusalem, the governing Jewish council. These and those who served with and around them were tasked with a great charge. We may put it this way: The Romans would offer them protection from outsiders and within, better infrastructure, roads, aqueducts, and such, if they would control their guerrilla fighters and other seditious types.

John's Gospel actually gives this the clearest expression. Some of those who had seen Jesus raise Lazarus from the dead "went and told the Pharisees . . . So the chief priests and the Pharisees called a meeting of the council, and said, 'What are we to do? This man is performing many signs. If we let him go on like this, everyone will believe in him, and the Romans will come and destroy both our holy place and our nation.' But one of them, Caiaphas, who was high priest that year, said to them, 'You know nothing at all! You do not understand that it is better for you to have one man die for the people than to have the whole nation destroyed'" (John 11:46–50).

Reading this passage and thinking about the predicament of the Jewish leaders, I have developed more sympathy for their plight. With Judas the Galilean and others on their minds, what Caiaphas advised was realistic. The Romans had, could, and would eventually come down on them like a ton of bricks.

Jesus was a troublemaker in their view. He stirred up the people. The Passover atmosphere was potentially combustible. The gathered throng of pilgrims, swelling Jerusalem two to three times its normal population, were there to celebrate the great feast of liberation from Egyptian slavery. At this time, the Roman garrison in Jerusalem was augmented by forces marching down from Caesarea on the Sea, the provincial Roman capital.

Marcus Borg has stirred my imagination with description of a cohort of Roman soldiers in full array: their steps in rhythm to drumbeat, their helmets glinting in the Palestinian sun, swords and spears rocking with footfall, and the clanking of body plates and shields. This was designed to impress with Roman might and to ward off fury by Passover enthusiasts.[3]

Eventually, Jesus was caught in the web of all these forces drawn tightly around him. His vision of the kingdom was too different and radical, not forceful enough, not observant enough, not politic enough. He could foresee the end coming. A cross was not hard to imagine. What is more, he had

---

3. Borg, *Jesus A New Vision*, 174. Borg and Crossan, *Last Week*, 3.

committed his life, not to a martyr's death, but to a kingdom of joy and justice and peace.

Hope and Grapple

The swirl of life around Jesus as seen in Matthew and the other Gospels raises a question of expectations. What did they expect him to be? What do we expect him to be?

Over against their expectations, Jesus would not be a military messiah, though there is evidence in the Gospels and Acts that his disciples wanted him to be. They were looking for a David-like leader to rally the people to throw out the Romans.

Over against those who practiced strict observance, he would not be a religious separatist. He was clearly leading a God-oriented movement. Yet the repeated inquiries of the scribes and Pharisees suggest that it took a while for them to ascertain the nature of his teaching and practice as different from their own.

Over against the Jewish leaders, the chief priests, Sadducees, and some Pharisees, the Jesus kingdom message and movement would not meld with the compromise they had struck with the Romans. Particularly around the Passover, during the procession from the Mount of Olives through the Kidron Valley and up to the Temple Mount, the motley, Hosanna-raising pilgrims made the leaders nervous. It didn't take much to stir Roman suspicion that the Sanhedrin and related functionaries had not done an adequate job of controlling Jewish zealotry.

Though "over against" can start a riot, it does not lead to a lasting faith. There was once a Friday night group which met at the home of dear friends with a spiritual gift for hospitality. Most of us there were disaffected members of a certain church. Naturally our conversation, which was often rich, partook of more than a few "over againsts."

After a few years, my wife and I came home one Friday, saying that it wasn't enough for us to be against something. We had to be for something. That was a turning point for me. Either I had to affirm where I was and stay with it, or I had to affirm another direction and pursue it.

To my mind, this is relevant today in both our churches and society. Denominations like my own have lost millions of members since the 1960s. We are discouraged by our changed profile in America from the mainstream to a mere tributary. It is quite clear that many have made decisions to reject us by conscious choice or indifference.

But "none of the above" is no more than a rejection of something. On those forms which ask for one's religious preference, one option is "none of the above." The numbers who check this box are increasing. They are referred to affectionately as "the nones."

In our churches, we may nurse our losses by doubling down on a kind of off-center identity. Some Presbyterians wear the kilt and tartan patterns, if not literally, in their heads, to hold onto a Scottish heritage. I will not attempt to connect other churches to particular cultural and/or ethnic identities. But they are there.

No one should be ashamed of where she comes from. Scotland is a wonderful place with a noble history, but Presbyterians enjoy other places of origin. To be a Christian is more than a coat of arms or a family crest. It is a deeper affirmation, expressing the stamp of God with Us on our human existence as in the cross with which we are signed at baptism.

Are the ways that a people double down on their identity or reject any by filling the "none" box an effort to get at something? Perhaps there is some gestating aspiration in circling the wagons or a deep longing for something greater than what's available. I hope so.

Furthermore, I pray that within the swirl of modern life, there is something other than cultural burnout and personal cynicism. Is there yet an "affirming flame" to light the way forward? Such longings and prayers take us to the heart of the prophetic nature of Jesus' ministry as he scanned the horizon.

Just a word about the overused term "prophetic." I believe that Jesus was thought to be a prophet by both enemies and friends (Matt 11:9–10; 13:57; 14:1–5; 21: 11, 45–46). And I believe that he was a prophet in several ways but specifically in his message and ministry toward the future.

A prophet like Jeremiah was not for people changing or acting justly to pass a litmus test for relevance. There were threatening signals of destruction on the horizon. An enemy "from the north" (Jer. 1:15) was on the move toward Jerusalem. Should Judah prepare and align with others to fight this aggressor, or should they, as Jeremiah preached, seek a renewed faithfulness to God and stand the ground God had provided?

Without telling the whole story, Jeremiah had one eye on the geopolitical reality of the Middle East and the other eye on God's providential care, even while armies clashed. Jesus, I believe, like Jeremiah, could see "the handwriting on the wall" (Dan 5) for Israel under the Romans. Jesus in Matthew gives us a vision of God with Us though armies clash, chaos reigns, the temple falls, and the people run for their lives.

A prophet is not merely a fortune-teller or soothsayer (that is, a forecaster of future events), but someone with a gift, even a divine gift, to perceive coming events and indicate the ways of God through them. Such ways may not be without catastrophe as they were with Jesus himself, but they are an alternative to the kingdoms of this world, that is, raw power and selfish motives.

Jesus' great affirmation was the kingdom of heaven, the vision of joy and justice, mercy and peace, that he proclaimed and lived. Though people of his day, including his own disciples, wanted him to go a different way, he pursued that divine and holy vision to the cross and up from the dead.

Today, it is that vision and life of Jesus that we should center our church around, in the context of larger society. It is both abundant life and a costly way. But it touches the heart of our existence like nothing else.

"Over against" our making Jesus the patron saint of whatever form or quality our churches take, the Savior is always calling us beyond what makes us merely feel good or safe to what really frees us for ourselves and others. At the same time, to be a prophetic church does not mean simply that we are always about change, whether a certain kind of pious behavior or a certain kind of social agenda. It means, rather, that we should read the gospel of Christ in a way that acknowledges both the tension and the distance between who and where he is and who and where we are. Thereby, we follow Christ in both our profession of faith and confession of wrong. In this way, we witness to Christ rather than to ourselves.

By not making ourselves the focus of God's mission in the world, we may shift our perceived purpose from a perch above others to a walk with them. Our partners in the world may not always be those who join our team. Rather, through our witness, they may find inspiration in the Christ who calls us all to remake the world according to the vision of the kingdom he proclaimed.

I call this "following with greater humility," and it consists of the divine favor that Jesus proclaimed in the Beatitudes. Through such grace for the likes of us, Jesus relocates us to our rightful place before God, with neighbors and toward ourselves. It is solid ground on which to stand as tall as befits our God-created humanity. And it saves us from the rickety ladder of pride the rungs of which are always unstable.

In very practical terms, the kingdom vision of Jesus Christ rivals and saves us from efforts that may be off the mark. As a church, we too often equate our losses in dollars, persons, and prestige with not being evangelistic enough or letting our morals slip. The one may have nothing to do with the other. In our efforts to rectify the ship, glossy church promotion and media-savvy communication may be like spitting in the wind.

Also, stringent moral denunciations and shrill social justice policies may neither address the underlying causes. Far too many have suffered abuse at the hands of the church. Our society's material surfeit may not be explained simply by greed. Grasping for and padding ourselves with things may mask fears and losses which lie beneath.

In delving for underlying causes, I am not suggesting that we side-step the need for self-control and social justice in a world that promotes greed and lust. Rather, that a more thoughtful presentation of the gospel can address how we may exit the swamp. For example, one does not help the addict by railing at drink and drugs. He or she has a much better lecture on that topic than we non-addicts can ever offer, a lecture often preached to oneself. What may actually find traction is when we offer the hope of recovery in practical terms with practical steps, informed by deeply spiritual ideals. If we do our homework in the gospel itself, resisting simplistic recipes for people's lives, I believe that God's Spirit will always work with us to draw followers to Christ. But if in any way we put ourselves out front of the message, we may obscure the Christ who needs no bullhorn, no gloss, no media wizardry.

As I grapple with following Christ in the modern church and society, I realize that traditionalists of most every kind have been knocked off their stride. I am no exception. Strategies for the church's continuing relevance in the modern world are topics that tempt some of us to peevishness. It is all too easy to bemoan any instantiation of church and to backslide into "none-of-the-above." Where does that leave me?

My plea is neither against creativity nor difference. Any authentic presentation of the gospel is worthy, no matter its dress or style, the word "authentic" being the key. Instead, I reject our modern fascination with the modes and manner of communication. Contrary to the modern aphorism, "The medium is not always the message." We live in a paradoxical relationship to the Savior. Our lives are wholly about the message, yet we are not saviors of anything.

A parable of Soren Kierkegaard says it better. "It happened that a fire broke out backstage in a theater. The clown came out to inform the public. They thought it was just a jest and applauded. He repeated his warning, they shouted even louder. So I think that the world will come to an end amid general applause from all the wits, who believe it is a joke."[4] In the world of the church, there is a difference between the message, the one true messenger, and we who follow, playing various parts. To obscure that distinction is to reverse roles, fall under the weight of our assignments, and to subvert the mission of Christ.

This begs for some comment about the call of Christ, human imperfection, and God with Us on the way. More on that later (Chapter 16, Hope and Grapple).

---

4. Kierkegaard, *Parables*, 3.

CHAPTER ELEVEN

The Content and Vision of the Kingdom

How we view the kingdom of heaven in Matthew and the Gospels generally takes us to the heart of Jesus' message. Whether or not we fix on those verses that emphasize its nearness or what is yet to come does not matter if we miss what the kingdom is about. Its formal definition is the rule of God or the reign of Christ, which means that the divine will shall prevail. But what is its substance or its content?

Here I grapple in hope of greater clarity. But what I am grappling with are the views of my upbringing, which are still prevalent across some churches today. Though many of us, thankfully, hear a different message from pulpits than what I heard in my youth, I'll wager there's yet a default setting at work when we read Matthew. Let's see if we can change it.

To the crux of my difficulty, let's consider this passage from Matthew 8. There Jesus says, "I tell you, many will come from east and west and will eat with Abraham and Isaac and Jacob in the kingdom of heaven, while the heirs of the kingdom will be thrown into the outer darkness, where there will be weeping and gnashing of teeth" (Matt 8:11–12).

"Weeping and gnashing of teeth" is a phrase, amended by outer darkness, that symbolizes separation and punishment. In chapter 8, Jesus speaks of a wider view of the kingdom wherein many will come to take part. But the children, the heirs of the kingdom, the people of Israel will be cast out. Any way one looks at it, it is a hard saying.

Furthermore, "weeping and gnashing of teeth" occurs only seven times in the four Gospels: six times in Matthew, one in Luke (Matt 8:12; 13; 42,50; 22:13; 24:51; 25:30; Luke 13:29). It graphically pictures the torments of gehenna, the fiery dump ground always burning in the Hinnom Valley near Jerusalem, which Jesus employs as an image of divine wrath. Gehenna and "weeping and gnashing" are never used in the same pericope, but the notion of torturous judgment is common to both.

It was this notion that filled my head as a child. The lurid picture of hell, as translated in the King James Version (most other versions have followed), was often portrayed to us as a negative incentive to act a certain way and steer clear of other paths. Often the context was about the steps to conversion. If we were not baptized, we would be condemned to hellfire. Preachers in those days did not mince words.

What is more, there was a scenario of salvation that had to do with landing in heaven or hell. "The soul of man [as the song goes] never dies." The soul being eternal, the question was, "Where will you [identifying the person with a disembodied soul/spirit] spend eternity?"

This life was thought to be merely a passage to one destination or the other. What happens here has more to do with a ledger of good or bad kept on each one of us, awaiting its exaction til the day of judgment. If we were baptized by immersion for the forgiveness of our sins, our marks were off to a good start. But we could always backslide. We did not believe in the "terrible" doctrine of "once saved, always saved." But as we began to relish a bit more security in God's grace, some of us jokingly said that our old belief was, "if saved, barely saved."

Passages such as the eleven that mention gehenna (7 in Matt, 3 in Mark, 1 in Luke) and the seven that picture "weeping and gnashing of teeth" (6 in Matt, 1 in Luke), were once laced through many a sermon. They were taught in relation to the kingdom which we thought was an equivalent of the church or heaven. Thus, hell and heaven were logically balanced opposites, one a place of eternal torment, the other a place of eternal bliss.

But the kingdom in Matthew is not merely a dwelling place of eternal bliss after this life. That is a complete distortion of its content. And if that is a complete distortion, the scenario collapses of this life as a mere passageway and testing ground for eternity. And if one side of the heaven/hell destination scheme collapses, what of the other? How are we to understand the lurid images, the scent of burning flesh, and the eternal cries of torment?

What Is the Kingdom about in Matthew?

"When John heard in prison what the Messiah was doing, he sent word by his disciples and said to him, 'Are you the one who is to come, or are we to wait for another?' Jesus answered them, 'Go and tell John what you hear and see: the blind receive their sight, the lame walk, the lepers are cleansed, the deaf hear, the dead are raised and the poor have good news preached to them. And blessed is anyone who takes no offense at me'" (Matt 11:2–6).

John in prison needed reassurance that Jesus was the one to come. The message Jesus sends back to John is a compilation of passages from Isaiah (29:18–19; 35:5–6; 61:1). Each is future-oriented in its outlook, an idealized future for sure, but nonetheless, an expectation of the world God would bring about. John's question and Jesus' response relate to the Messiah, the one anointed to usher in God's future.

And when the title "messiah" or "christ" (its Greek translation) is used, a kingdom is always in reference. The kingdom of heaven, as Matthew mostly refers to it (in Mark and Luke, it is the kingdom of God), probably indicates the Jewish reticence to say the name God, though Matthew uses "kingdom of God" four times. Not to get lost in word usage, my point is that the Messiah or the Christ is never without a kingdom.

Heaven in Matthew, as in "our father who art in heaven" (Matt 6:9), is the dwelling place of God. Jesus in Matthew refers to heaven as both the sky and God's habitation as in "consider the birds of heaven . . . your father in heaven feeds them" (Matt 6:26). But heaven is never up, up, and away. It is always related to the earth. Therefore, preaching about the kingdom in Matthew is about God's transformation of earth into its heavenly ideal, 'on earth as it is in heaven" (Matt 6:10).

In more technical language, "heaven" is a term for the realm of God's transcendent reality, that is, beyond creation as such. Matthew's Gospel is about God with Us, the one who makes God's self and will known on earth and proclaims God's kingdom. This same Jesus of Nazareth is the one who embodies the beginning of the future to come.

For John to hear in prison about the works of the Messiah was a kind of freedom for the captive (Isa 61:1). It was an old vision brought forward and renewed in the person and work of Jesus, the Savior. But this whole portrait in language of the kingdom was not about a spiritual realm unrelated to earthly existence.

The Angle of Vision

I once heard on Public Broadcasting the Dutch-born Long Island artist Willem de Kooning say how he saw what to paint. "I am a slipping glimpser," were close to his exact words. He interpreted them just enough for me to infer that De Kooning painted what he saw while off-balance or even on the way down. Not literally so, at least not in every case, but slipping, off-balance nonetheless.

The thought intrigued me, and it relates to Matthew. Consider three passages almost in sequence. Headed in some Bibles, "The Beginning of the Galilean Ministry," Jesus moves from Nazareth to make his home in Capernaum by the Sea. Then follows the quote from Isaiah, "Land of Zebulon and land of Naphtali, the way of the sea, across the Jordan, Galilee of the gentiles, the people who sat in darkness have seen a great light, upon those who sit in the region and shadow of death, light has dawned" (Matt 4:15–16; Isa 9:1–2).

Immediately following, "from then, Jesus began to preach and to say, 'repent, for the kingdom of heaven is near'" (Matt 4:17). The combination is striking: "light dawning upon the gentiles" and "the kingdom of heaven is near."

There is then the call of Peter, Andrew, James, and John from their nets and boats, whereupon Jesus goes about the whole of Galilee, "preaching the good news of the kingdom and healing all diseases" (Matt 4:23). As Martin Dibelius made so clear, Jesus' healings are signs of the kingdom.[1]

Whereupon that great crowd, many newly healed, follows Jesus up on the mountain. He takes his place, and "opening his mouth, taught them saying, 'Blessed are the poor in spirit, for theirs is the kingdom of heaven'" (Matt 5:2–3).

Who does Matthew identify in relation to the kingdom? Gentiles who dwelt in darkness, those tormented by disease and possessed of demons, and the poor in spirit. In contrast to the well in body and the ritually pure of Israel, those "who have no need of a physician" (Matt 9:12), there were those who might be "slipping glimpsers." Foreigners, the demon possessed, the sick and punished for their sins, the downtrodden poor of the land, not strictly observant, these are they for whom Jesus proclaimed the good news of the kingdom and on whom Jesus' heart fixed with compassion (Matt 9).

Elsewhere in Matthew it is children (Matt 18, 19) whom Jesus raises up. "Unless you turn and become like a child, you shall not enter the kingdom of heaven" (Matt 18:3). And in chapter 19, "Receive the children and do not forbid them to come to me, for of such is the kingdom of heaven" (Matt 19:14).

The "least in faith," "the lost sheep," "the brother (or sister) who sins" are featured figures in Matthew 18. In Matthew 25, "The king will say to those on his right hand, those who are blessed by my father shall inherit the kingdom prepared from the foundation of the world. For I was hungry and

---

1. Dibelius, *Jesus*, 87.

you gave me to eat, thirsty . . . to drink; a stranger and you welcomed me; naked and you clothed me; weak and you cared for me; in prison and you visited me . . . as you did [this] to one of the least of these who are members of my family, you did [it] to me" (Matt 25:34–40).

The angle of vision from which to see the kingdom belongs to those who cry out in need. None is greater than the Canaanite woman, whose plea for her daughter in the face of Jesus' stern rebuke shines brightest of all. "O woman, great is your faith" (Matt 15:28).

It was not enough for Jesus in Matthew to merely display them as an honor guard, waving the colors of their kingdom sightings. He moved from the cast and the drama to encounter the audience. "Come to me all you that are weary and are carrying heavy burdens, and I will give you rest. Take my yoke upon you and learn from me; for I am gentle and humble in heart and you shall find rest for your souls. For my yoke is easy, and my burden is light" (Matt 11:28–30).

Not only does the Savior speak to the humble and lowly, he is among them as one who is humble and lowly. He embodies the kingdom that he portrays in his teachings and healings. We draw near the kingdom as we attend to the least of these. We aspire to the kingdom as we feel our limits to heal and save ourselves.

Hope and Grapple

In Jesus there is a radical openness that carries out God's mission with Israel of being a light to the Gentiles. The Pharisees asked the disciples, "'Why does your teacher eat with tax collectors and sinners?' Jesus, overhearing, said, 'Those who are well [or strong], have no need of a physician, but those who are sick. Go and learn what this means, *I desire mercy and not sacrifice*, for I came not to call the righteous but sinners" (Matt 9: 11–13, my translation). We need not venture from Matthew to hear and see Jesus opening the new world of the kingdom to women, children, tax collectors, sinners, non-observant Jews, Gentiles. The rest of the New Testament follows him in this. Paul wrote to the Romans, "Therefore, welcome one another, just as Christ has welcomed you, to the glory of God" (Rom. 15:7). In short, a radical openness and submission to God's kingdom means following the openness and submission of the Kingdom Messiah. The kingdom of heaven in Jesus' person and proclamation is about the beachhead, the beginnings of a new creation of heaven and earth, not an escape hatch from earth to Paradise Island.

In the movie, *Mary Magdalene* there is a quite plausible depiction of how difficult it was for a woman to follow Jesus in the way that the male disciples did. The roles for women were set in that society. They were not to talk to men in public. They were to sit separately in the synagogue. They were to get married, have children, and generally submit to the men in their lives and men in positions of authority. But what if God called a woman to follow the Savior by journeying with him, attending his words, healing, teaching and even baptizing? Such a person would be ostracized and painfully so.

Jesus in *Mary Magdalene* speaks a portion of these verses from Matthew 10: "Think not that I came to bring peace on the earth; I did not come to bring peace but a sword. For I came to divide a man against his father, a daughter against her mother, a bride against her mother-in-law, and the enemies of a man will be those of his own household. He who loves father or mother more than me is not worthy of me, and he who loves son or daughter more than me is not worthy of me" (Matt 10:34–37).

This is not a passage in opposition to "blessed are the peacemakers." It is a reflection of actual life wherein following Jesus counters cultural beliefs about the role of women and men too, for that matter. Jesus might have been accused of not supporting family values.

Back to Mary Magdalene, Matthew tells us that there were other women, in fact many women, who had followed Jesus from Galilee to serve him (Matt 27:55). In all four of the evangelists' stories of the resurrection, the women were first at the empty tomb. They were first to be addressed by angels and the risen Lord. And they were instructed to tell the others, the male disciples. All this in a society that did not believe that women were credible witnesses because they were too dimwitted to sort through evidence and discern truth. For example, when Mary Magdalene, Joanna, Mary the mother of James, and the others reported the words of the messengers at the empty tomb, "He is not here. He is risen," the men said in their presence, "'These words are an idle tale,' and they did not believe them" (Luke 24:11).

But truly the women were the first witnesses to the resurrection. The great bishop and poet John Donne called them "supernumerary apostles, apostles to the apostles."[2] Though the gnostic literature, such as the Gospel of Mary Magdala, which was one source for the movie, holds a special place for women, the canonical Gospels elevate women beyond their set roles in the culture. Jesus' hard-sounding words about separating families may refer to actual events when women, among others, began to go against the grain of customs and teaching to walk with Jesus. It would not be the first time,

---

2. Donne, *Devotions*, 40.

nor the last, that women especially have been abused for moving beyond accepted roles.

In the church today, we are still divided as to how open we should be to persons who do not fit certain cultural norms. Some still argue Scripture against women taking roles in church leadership, while others cannot come round to an acceptance of LGBTQ persons.

In this context, we must remind ourselves of the difference between grace as God's favor and grace as forgiveness. The former is prior. God accepts whoever abides human skin and how the desires of a person are oriented. These, we now know, are not choices, but genetics. Persons do not suffer divine rejection for who they are in their own skin.

As to controlling our passions, Christians, adherents of other religions, and teachers of morality generally agree we should. In what may feel to some of us like a new world, it might be good if older pastors like me listened more and pronounced less. We might be surprised to learn that LGBTQ persons, if we are not among them, have developed some excellent thoughts along these lines.

We might draw an analogy from missiology. In missions, we have had to learn that the churches of Europe and North America must be open to churches elsewhere across the globe to allow the gospel to plant itself in new cultures. That is, we must be open to the work of the Holy Spirit in making Christ known and present.

Beyond matters of human sexuality, there are many ways that persons are different. Aborigine, African, Arab, Asian, Caucasian, Hispanic, Latino, native persons such as Native Americans and the Tribals of India; I mention only some, but not nearly all the peoples of earth. To draw up a list is nothing more than an indicator.

The old survey-box racial/ethnic persons as other than white strikes me as strange. All of us, including those who check "white," are of some race and ethnicity. Today many persons are of mixed race. Many families are mixed race. To do a serious study of human DNA, we are learning that DNA profiles across the African continent alone are more diverse than between Africa and Europe, for example. The whole human race is a mixed race, leading to an excellent question: What is race exactly?[3]

Nonetheless, we are each part of certain cultures. Language is a primary delimiting factor of culture. For example, blue-eyed, blonde-haired persons whose native language is Arabic and whose upbringing is among Arabs are Arabs. Looks aside, we are persons of culture, though some may

---

3. Kolbert, *National Geographic*, 29–41.

be cultural polyglots, as the actor Peter Ustinov thought of himself (though he used the word "mongrel").

And yet, we live in times when fear and the politics of fear push us to clash culturally. In the face of such fearmongering, it is necessary for civil societies to, at least, tolerate cultural diversity. Beyond tolerance, certain quarters of the church and society celebrate difference and diversity. To my mind, that is a gospel impulse drawn from Israel's role as a light to the nations and Jesus' great commission to take the gospel into all the world (all nations).

But when diversity moves from our heads to our neighborhoods, it is not easy to do. I cannot get inside another's skin to understand fully what it is to be other than a lightish brown male (thought to be white) who grew up in Texas, attended college in Arkansas, and spent 46 years in New York and New Jersey before retiring to North Carolina.

Even so, there are aspects of my journey which help me to understand separation, dislocation, and alienation. I know almost instinctively, certainly experientially, that my own woundedness and vulnerability are similar to that of others. I grew up in a single-parent family before that phrase was in use. My father died a few weeks after my fifteenth birthday. My mother and I did not have much, but we managed, thanks to her hard work and loving care of me. These are aspects of my life which can serve as a lens to appreciate persons who have different stories. But I cannot know exactly what it is like to be someone other than me. None of us can.

Unfortunately a certain smugness can cloud our attempts to value others in their difference. Anyone can look down on another's inability to understand what it is like to be "you" or "me." However, such smugness will not allow us to walk the road together, a road our world so desperately needs the human race to travel.

Not perfect understanding, but learning how to get along as different, represents to me the closet of shoes we need to try on. I think of this learning as "leaning into one another." We cannot be one another, but we can "lean in" as persons who listen carefully.

Listening is sometimes tricky. When I have opened my mouth to test if I have got something right, I have put my foot in it and felt like my head was bitten off. But that is but a wee death on the way to life.

To assist us, there are many programs and schools and special teachers, not to mention a number of houses of worship, which are practicing "leaning in." This is simply the term I use to describe this attitude. Others probably have better words to describe this form of learning.

Traveling with Matthew, it is my strong belief that by learning to stand arm-in-arm before God and with the least among us, we can best learn difference and community. We do not all have to sit in the same seat to gather around the same table. Especially when we learn that the host and table do not belong to us, but to God with Us, can we learn that our places are secure in our difference, and we are wonderfully made for one another.

CHAPTER TWELVE

Jesus and the Torn Temple Curtain

READING AND UNDERSTANDING SCRIPTURE is a practice with an artistic flavor. Depending on the particular passage, one must ask, What picture faces the reader? Is it of creation, the exodus, the wilderness wanderings or the Davidic monarchy? What about each seems important to the author(s)? How does each portion of Scripture speak of God's role in what takes place? Much more can be said about biblical interpretation, but this is enough to suggest how we as pilgrims should tread this holy ground.

Traveling with Matthew, we have been pursuing themes and how the author weaves them through the story of Jesus of Nazareth. As noted, God with Us is a major theme, if not the major theme. Therefore, key to our reading Matthew is asking how God is with us, not only where that thematic phrase is explicit, but wherever on the page Jesus is present.

I suggest that the art of understanding Matthew is following the rise and fall of its landscape. By allowing Matthew to guide us, we walk by the light of Christ placed on the lampstand to illuminate the whole house. In this way, we allow the light to go with us through the shadows rather than camping in the dark. How we read Scripture is not much different to how we go at life. Do we allow the dark to make a home within our hearts and minds, an address of despair and meaninglessness? Or do we trust the light to illuminate those who sit in darkness and bring the magi to Bethlehem?

This principle of moving from the known to the unknown applies in a variety of Matthew locations. We may see it most clearly in Matthew 24, which admittedly is confusing.

The subject is Jesus' saying about the temple, what will happen to it, the coming of the Son of Man, and the close of the age. The language is apocalyptic, which literally means "revelation." That is an ironic designation for this literary genre because apocalyptic use of images and symbols is anything but straightforward.

I am influenced here by the biblical scholar and theologian G.B. Caird's *The Language and Imagery of the Bible*. About the apocalyptic style he observed, "When an author writes a book (such as Daniel or Revelation) consisting wholly or mainly of symbols, there is a prima facie case for not supposing him to be a literalist."[1] And yet, modern readers, both sophisticated scholars and first-time Bible students, have assumed that Revelation, for example, is literally describing the furniture of heaven. Therefore, some dismiss it entirely as nonsense while others go to Home Depot to match the wall paper with the couches. Is there not a reading on the continuum somewhere between sheer nonsense and helping God with the color scheme? Let's give it a go.

Jesus and the Temple

To understand what the Gospels say about Jesus and the temple, we need to reach back to two great passages. Second Samuel 7 recalls that the Lord has moved about with the people in "a tent and a tabernacle" (2 Sam 7:6). Speaking through the prophet Nathan, the Lord says to David, "I will appoint a place for my people Israel and will plant them, so that they may live in their own place, and be disturbed no more" (2 Sam. 7:10).

Nathan goes on to say that the Lord will raise up offspring for David and will establish his kingdom (2 Sam 7:12–13). In the concluding and key verse, Nathan says to David, "Your house and your kingdom shall be made sure forever before me; your throne shall be established forever" (2 Sam 7:16).

Following the story as it lived in the people's memory, we must turn to 2 Chronicles 5, for there, King Solomon, David's son, completed the temple as promised. To its inner sanctuary the priests brought the ark of the covenant in which resided the two tablets of the law. "There was nothing in the ark except the two tablets that Moses put there at Horeb, where the Lord made a covenant with the people of Israel after they came out of Egypt" (2 Chr 5:10).

Then the priests vacated the most holy place. The singers and other musicians round about raised a song of praise in the words, "For the Lord is good, for his steadfast love endures forever" (2 Chr 5:13). Whereupon "The house of the Lord was filled with a cloud, so that the priests could not stand

---

1. Caird, *Language and Imagery*, 262.

to minister because of the cloud; for the glory of the Lord filled the house of God" (2 Chr 5:14).

The temple was Israel's symbol of an everlasting kingdom promised to David, and the gem of the Lord's glory that resided therein. When in 587 BCE the Babylonians destroyed the temple and took many of the Jewish leaders away into captivity, a crisis of faith occurred (Ps. 137). This crisis should also indicate the importance for them of rebuilding the temple once they returned from exile in Babylon, a concern that occupies a good portion of the Old Testament.

And it should speak to us of the passion felt by the Maccabees when Antiochus Epiphanes desecrated the temple in 167 and 165 BCE. The war and victory that followed led to a cleansing and rededication of the temple in 164 BCE, celebrated each year by the Feast of Dedication, or Hanukkah.

But it was not this temple that stood in Jesus' day, rather, the temple built by Herod the Great. Though controversial in many ways, Herod was, without a doubt, an amazing builder. And his temple was the closest in grandeur to Solomon's. So, it should come as no surprise that Jesus' disciples (Matt 24) expressed such wonder, like tourists at the Taj Mahal, as they oohed and aahed about the temple's magnificent buildings.

With that story in hand, we need to retrieve another, Jeremiah 7:1–4. "The word that came to Jeremiah from the Lord: Stand in the gate of the Lord's house, and proclaim there this word, and say, Hear the word of the Lord, all you people of Judah, you that enter these gates to worship the Lord. Thus says the Lord of hosts, the God of Israel: Amend your ways and your doings, and let me dwell with you in this place. Do not trust in these deceptive words: 'This is the temple of the Lord, the temple of the Lord, the temple of the Lord.'"

It must suffice to say that Jeremiah was, from the beginning of his prophetic work, warning Judah against an enemy from the north. This was God's judgment upon the people for their idolatrous rebellion against the divine covenant (Jer 1:14–16). With a message that was hard to hear, Jeremiah was exhorting them to align with this flow of history and to submit to the Babylonian aggressors rather than seek alliances with Egypt or Assyria to oppose them (Jer. 2:18).

In this context, Jeremiah called for repentance, a change of heart rather than military resistance. They should not trust that the divine presence would always abide in the temple when the people had turned their backs on God. Jeremiah represents a different vision of the covenant between God and Israel than that struck with David.

The temple was important for both visions, both covenants, as it was for Jesus. But Jesus bore more kinship to the weeping Jeremiah than to those who sought to maintain the temple and its place at all costs. Not Babylon but another nation, even stronger, occupied Israel in the days of Jesus and Matthew.

Like a Jeremiah, standing in the gates of the temple, warning against deceptive loyalties, Jesus taught and took action against the chief priests, the Sadducees, and likely some Pharisees. They had made a deal with Rome to keep their own radical dagger- and sword-wielders from insurrection. (Though not explicitly stated, this agreement is indicated by John 11:45–53.) In return, the Romans, unlike the Seleucid dynasty before them, were to leave in place the temple as the center of Torah observance and ritual sacrifices. Though from this distance, we may imagine that the priestly class had wrested forgiveness from God and assumed that role for themselves, Jesus never criticized them for doing so.

After all, we have noted the biblical precedent they could recite. God had promised David an everlasting kingdom and a house for the divine presence. The prophets Isaiah and Micah had advanced the promise to when "in days to come the mountain of the Lord's house shall be established as the highest of the mountains, and shall be raised above the hills; all the nations shall stream to it" (Isa 2:2; Mic. 4:1–2). Jerusalem with its holy temple was thought to be the center of the earth and eventually the gathering place of all God's people.

But Jesus in Matthew, following John the Baptist, did not view the great symbols of Israel of his day, the temple, Torah, land and people as quite so fixed. They were never immoveable objects in a no-matter-what relationship with God. Either the people must turn back to God, or God must intervene for the people. The status quo would not do. And when the weight of wrong pressed too strong, the balance of redemption shifted in the person of Jesus to what God alone could do.

Over Against the Temple, a Recentering of God's Purpose

As Jesus and the disciples were leaving the temple, "they showed him its great buildings, but Jesus said, 'Do you see all these? Truly, I say to you, not one stone will be left here upon another which will not be destroyed'" (Matt 24:1–2).

Then they moved from the Temple Mount down through the Kidron Valley and up the Mount of Olives. From that vantage point where even today the Temple Mount, minus the temple, can be seen most clearly, the disciples ask for an explanation. "Tell us when all these things will be, and what will be the sign of your coming and the close of the age" (Matt 24:3).

These two questions serve as headings for the division of the chapter that follows. One, "Tell us when all these things will be." That is, tell us when not one stone will be left upon another of the temple buildings.

We may call this the category of "the known." To those who read Matthew about 80 to 95 CE, the destruction of the temple was so recent (70 CE) that the olfactory memory of its smoking debris had not abated. And verses 4–31 are both reminiscent of the horror of it and a call to get through the ensuing chaos.

The days would be full of great deception. False christs and false prophets would put forth their claims. Remember that "christ" is not only specific to Jesus, but a general term for anyone who takes on the mantle to lead and save Israel. Wars would rage among nations. Earthquakes and famine would bring devastation everywhere. Lest the chaos obscure and destroy faith, Jesus encourages patience unto the end. As a sign of hope, he says, "this gospel of the kingdom will be proclaimed in the whole inhabited world as a witness to all the nations, and then the end will come" (Matt 24:4–14).

It seems that the chapter has come to a climax with talk of the end, but it hasn't. We enter another phase of this apocalyptic vision. Only this time, the images seem to be drawn from the suffering of those caught within the destruction of Jerusalem. Jesus and/or the narrator tells it as if inside the experience of those who went through it. "Those in Jerusalem will flee to the mountains." "If on the housetop, don't bother to come down." Jump and run, I presume. "If in the field, don't go back to get your clothes" (Matt 24:17–18). "Woe to the pregnant and those nursing" (Matt 24:19). At that time "great will be the affliction such as it has never been from the beginning of the world until now nor ever will be" (Matt 24:20). Again this is followed by confusion as to where the Christ is in this holocaust, with some announcing that he is in the desert. Others, that he is secreted in a chamber somewhere.

As if this is not enough, "the sun and moon will not shine; the stars will fall from the heavens, and the power of the heavens will be shaken" (Matt 24: 29). "Then the Son of Man will come on the clouds of heaven with power and great glory" (Matt 24: 30).

Reeling from the rich and lurid imagery of the vision, we make our way through it like hearing a Mahler symphony, with two or three expectations of a conclusion before it finally resounds. In the next two verses, surely we have reached a climax. "Truly I say to you that this generation will not pass away until all these things have occurred. Heaven and earth will pass away, but my words will not pass away" (Matt 24:34–35).

Momentous things have been told. Have they been about the recent past, the far away future, the end of time and space? We are not exactly sure. But a clue is that "this generation will not pass away until all these things have occurred." I believe that we can hang our hats on that. However much we run upon the future and then back away, however much we face the deception of false christs and prophets and yet are given the order to persist, the horrifying nightmare of the vision depicts the end of an era, not the end of the space/time universe we know.

Somehow through it all the words of Jesus abide though everything else has been shaken. Words in this reference are not merely the words of the Bible as if the devotion and sacrifice of great scholars and missionaries will keep generating them. Jesus' words outlast print and paper, heaven and earth. They partake of the eternal. It is as if Matthew is saying, God with Us has not been vanquished with the siege of Jerusalem and the destruction of the temple. Where we have formerly looked for the presence of God, one stone does not remain upon another. A second coming of God's presence must redirect our gaze and our hope.

The Center Cannot Hold

These lines from W. B. Yeats's poem, "The Second Coming," share similar features with the apocalyptic picture of chaos in Matthew 24. In fact, Yeats's poem itself has an apocalyptic feel to it:

> Turning and turning in the widening gyre
> The falcon cannot hear the falconer;
> Things fall apart; the centre cannot hold;
> Mere anarchy is loosed upon the world,
> The blood-dimmed tide is loosed, and everywhere
> The ceremony of innocence is drowned;
> The best lack all conviction, while the worst
> Are full of passionate intensity.[2]

Yeats wrote the poem in 1919. The horror of WWI and perhaps the troubles of Ireland were its background. I have not quoted the whole poem here because I am not trying to interpret it except to say that it resembles in genre the language of another time when the center had come apart. Again it is *how* a poem means as much if not more than *what* it means. Both apocalyptic writings relate to actual catastrophic events. Both treat the second coming as a new beginning in the midst of chaos. Both leave a

---

2. Yeats, *Selected Poems*, 91.

question mark about the nature of that new beginning. Both grip the human imagination powerfully about something quite beyond us as we go through times of terror.

Returning to the first century from the twentieth, Matthew likens Jesus to a new temple. Responding to the Pharisees who have criticized his disciples for picking grain to eat on the Sabbath, he queries them, "Have you not read in the law that on the Sabbath the priests in the temple break the sabbath and yet are guiltless? I tell you something greater than the temple is here . . . The Son of Man is lord of the Sabbath" (Matt 12: 5–6, 8). Literally the Greek has it, "Greater than the temple is here." I take it that the reference is to the one who is also lord of the Sabbath.

Like the other three Gospels, Matthew takes Jesus to the temple where he cleanses it. "Then Jesus entered the temple and drove out all who were selling and buying in the temple, and he overturned the tables of the money changers and the seats of those who sold doves. He said to them, 'It is written, "My house shall be called a house of prayer;" but you are making it a den of robbers'" (Matt 21:12–13).

A casual reading might imagine Jesus is upset with a commercial, profit-making operation that devalues the proper use of sacred space. But Jesus did not engage in prophetic action because he disapproved of a gift shop in a corner of the cathedral. What he disapproved of was the whole sacrificial system of changing profane currency for temple coinage, so that the people could buy animals to be sacrificed for their sins.

N. T. Wright reminds us what the temple was: "The place where YHWH lived and ruled in the midst of Israel, and where, through the sacrificial system which reached its climax in the great festivals, he lived in grace, forgiving them, restoring them, and enabling them to be cleansed of defilement and so to continue as his people."[3] Like Jeremiah before him, Jesus upsets all of that.

Then he tells his disciples that the temple is about to be destroyed (Matt 24:3). In John's Gospel, Jesus, following his gesture of cleansing the temple, responds to a question as to what he meant by his fury in their holy space. Jesus says, "Destroy this temple, and in three days, I will raise it up" (John 2: 19).

While Jesus was on the cross, some taunted him saying, "You who would destroy the temple and build it in three days, save yourself" (Matt 27:40). John interprets Jesus' saying to mean that "he was speaking of the temple of his body" (John 2:21). The upshot is that Jesus and the temple are held together in comparison.

---

3. Wright, *New Testament*, 224.

But Matthew, Mark, and Luke extend the comparison in a special way. "Jesus again crying with a loud voice gave up his spirit. And behold the curtain of the temple was split in two from top to bottom" (Matt 27:50; Mark 15:38; Luke 23:45). The one on the cross "came to give his life as a ransom for many" (Matt 20:28; Mark 10:45).

The torn curtain contrasts with Jesus' spilt blood. One represents the former place of forgiveness while the other is now the embodiment of forgiveness. Matthew and the Gospels recenter Israel. Matthew particularly recenters Israel and the new Israel around God with Us.

To the reader, I have not forgotten that second part of the disciples' question while they sat on the Mount of Olives, minds fixed across the valley on Jerusalem. "What will be the sign of your coming and the close of the age?" (Matt 24:3.) Some things will be painfully evident, and yet a future remains unknown. Only the father knows (Matt 24:36). We are to live toward that future with anticipation as if our whole lives counted on it (Matt 24:37–51).

And yet, Scripture does not give us a straightforward, prosaic description of what that future holds. Revelation supplies us with an amazing vision. The Apostle Paul echoes Isaiah 64: 4 when he says, "What no eye has seen, nor ear heard, nor the human heart conceived, what God has prepared for those who love him" (1 Cor 2:9). Except through poetic imagination and longings of the heart, there is not much said about the exact nature of God's future. Strangely, what Jesus specifies as unknown to mortals, even to himself, has become, for some, a cottage industry to discover what only God knows.

I do not make light here. I totally understand the longing of the heart toward God's future. Once in a Bible class when discussion turned to these matters I asked, "Have you enjoyed life at its best?" Heads nodded. "To me that says God can create a world that satisfies us." I am not worried that I or we will be disappointed.

Rather, I accept Matthew's final promise on Jesus' lips. "I will be with you to the close of the age" (Matt 28:20). God is with us. Is it not enough that we are to be with God in some future of God's making? Longing for that, I don't think we'll be disappointed.

Hope and Grapple

As I write this on All Saints Day, I turn to the future, the future to which Christ directs us. In Matthew 24, Jesus promises that the Son of Man will come in the midst of catastrophe and chaos. These horrors are depicted as if the very order of creation has come undone.

Jeremiah, before Jesus, had likened the reign of social injustice to the return of primeval chaos. "I looked on the earth, and lo, it was waste and void; and to the heavens, and they had no light. I looked on the mountains, and lo, they were quaking, and all the hills moved to and fro. I looked, and lo, there was no one at all, and all the birds of the air had fled. I looked, and lo, the fruitful land was a desert, and all its cities were laid in ruins before the Lord, before his fierce anger.

"For thus says the Lord: The whole land shall be a desolation; yet I will not make a full end. Because of this the earth shall mourn, and the heavens above grow black; for I have spoken, I have purposed; I have not relented nor will I turn back" (Jer. 4:23–28).

A world without birds puts me in mind of Rachel Carson's *Silent Spring* (1962). Some credit her as the beginning of the modern environmental movement. And I believe the science to be true that unless we become better stewards of the earth, it will not sustain life as it has. Even such warnings do not intend to paralyze us with fear but to propel us to action.

As for our assumption that the poetry of the language (foreboding as it is) refers to a literal end of all nature, we may have missed the power of Jesus' words in Matthew. God is yet coming though our individual worlds and the world as we know it are falling apart.

This has certainly occurred on history's broad plain. It has inhabited the human heart and mind with chaos in nightmare and abject sorrow. Yet, even these terrors of history and anguish of the self are not beyond the transforming presence and power of the one coming.

Only God can make an ultimate end of what God has created. This ultimate is beyond our plotting. It is also beyond our imagining. We may benefit from the reminder that in Christian theology, creation is all that God has made. The planet earth is not creation's limit. What we do to this earth, as destructive as it may be, is not the end of creation or the Creator.

And though Matthew's language of the ultimate coming is full of warning, I cannot dissolve Jesus' admonition "to watch" (Matt 24: 42) into an existential mood of terror, a perpetual insecurity, a failure of nerve (loss of faith) and uncertainty as to which side one will be on. At our worst, we Christians have gleefully looked upon the damned. But my psychological make-up has been to feel their lot.

Matthew needs Paul. The canon is a unit. "If God is for us, who can be against us?" (Rom 8: 31.) Does Matthew overwhelm his own theme of Jesus, Emmanuel, God with Us?

The evangelist does not, unless we allow the way that Jesus exhorts us to endure to overshadow the compassion he embodies and the invitation he extends. At the end of the day, judgment does not overwhelm mercy. Light yet shines in the darkness as in the beginning. Resurrection to life gets us through the dark night of the cross and the tomb. The Savior's "Come unto me . . ." dawns for "the weary and the heavy laden . . ." with temporal and eternal rest (Matt 11: 28–30).

CHAPTER THIRTEEN

Belonging and Identity

WE HAVE BEEN CONSIDERING how Matthew recenters the people and purpose of God around Jesus, in contrast to the temple. Centers and boundaries or circumferences, to stay geometrically accurate, shape identities. The image may have taken a jump from geometry to peoples and systems theory, but the leap is not hard to follow.

That which centers us is also that which keeps us and identifies us. Take a family of biological or adopted members. The center is, perhaps, a family name(s) and a certain cultural heritage. With that there is a dwelling place and a storyline. Physical traits, the relationship of parents/guardians, what happens or does not around the table, expectations of the children, family customs and habits, beliefs that are modeled and/or taught, all compose the centerpiece.

How the family relates to others and other viewpoints gets at the boundaries. Is the family insular or hospitable? What does the family think of the friends the children bring home? Should one go away to college, stay at home, or go to work to support the family rather than take courses to better oneself? How about serving church, nation, community? Who may one bring home as a prospective bride or groom? Do the parents threaten the children with headaches, heart attacks, silence, even shunning over differences with family values such as politics, religion, ethical views, and vocational choices?

The system of sacrifices and a certain set of practices of the Law of Moses composed the center of Israel's life in the temple. Not the least was a belief that God's presence was uniquely there.

With the destruction of the temple on the horizon, Jesus in Matthew begins to occupy the place once held by that sacred structural symbol in

Jerusalem. Related to the tension in the story is, most likely, the fact that Jesus came from Nazareth in Galilee. As we have noted about Galilee, there was a greater mix of Jews and Gentiles there than in Judea. At some distance from Jerusalem in the south, the synagogue in Galilee, like synagogues in the diaspora, had become the center of religious life.

In the later Mishnah, there is a saying similar to Matthew 18: 20, "Where two or three are gathered in my name, there I am in their midst." The Mishnah has it, "Where two or three gather to study Torah, the Shekinah [divine presence] rests upon them."[1] Was each drawing on the same source, or at least, a similar pattern of thought? We know for sure that the Matthew version is in a chapter that makes references to the church, and for that reason, most likely Matthew has read the early church backward into Jesus' day. Nonetheless, the emphasis is on Jesus' presence as center of the communal life. Related to the study of Torah and the Mishnah, is Jesus also thought by Matthew to be the divine word?

Back when the temple still existed, Jews were expected to do their best to travel regularly to Jerusalem for the great feasts, Passover, Pentecost and Tabernacles. Even at some distance, as N.T. Wright has observed, the boundary fences between Jewish and Gentile identity were to be kept mended, which were the practices of circumcision (a sign of ethnic purity), keeping Sabbath (regular devotion to God), and ritual purity (such as keeping kosher tables). Though Jews had dealings with Gentiles, particularly in Galilee and the diaspora, I follow N.T. Wright that "there is good warrant for believing that most Jews most of the time felt that fidelity to the Torah implied non-association as far as one could manage it."[2]

What must be reemphasized is the reason for strict observance of the Law. Keeping distance from Gentiles represented concern for Jewish identity and devotion to the God of Israel. The same is true of the religious observances and marks of Jewish purity. Assimilation into the Gentile world was a prevalent concern and an occasional threat. One only has to consider in Scripture the Assyrian captivity and that nation's practice of assimilating captives, hence the lost tribes (722 BCE).

But even after the more tolerant Babylonian captivity, the returning exiles were passionate about dedicating themselves to rebuilding the temple. And Torah observance took a more radical turn. Ezra and Nehemiah in the Old Testament are replete with this renewed emphasis. Strict obedience was highlighted by forbidding intermarriage with foreigners, along with other assiduous practices of distinction in keeping the Law.

1. Wright, *New Testament*, 228.
2. Wright, *New Testament*, 239.

But for those in Jesus' day, the most recent memory was of the Maccabees and what led to their revolt. We have considered the desecration of the temple by Antiochus Epiphanes (167, 165 BCE). It is no coincidence that during this period, the Pharisees came into being, a movement that practiced strict observance of the Torah. As to the name "Pharisees" itself, Wright calls attention to the fuzziness of its etymology.[3]

But we cannot argue with the spirit of those times that gave birth to a renewed separatism. Mattathias, the patriarch of the Hasmoneans, draws a line in the sand in First Maccabees: "If we all do as our kindred have done and refuse to fight with the Gentiles for our lives and our ordinances, they will quickly destroy us from the earth" (1 Macc 2: 40). Separation from the Gentiles, keeping the boundaries, came to the fore when Jews were violently persecuted, drawn into the fight and/or felt a keen pressure to sacrifice their identity.

Following the lead of the New Testament scholar Gerd Theissen, who has read the Gospels with a sociologist's eye, the events of the first century in Palestine precipitated another crisis in Jewish identity.[4] According to the Gospels, Jesus is thick in the middle of it. Moving from sociology to faith, Jesus adds to the mix a divine calling that includes a prophet's rereading of sacred history for the present. Matthew accents this calling with stories of his birth, baptism, and transfiguration (as does Luke with all three and Mark with baptism and transfiguration). Each and together portray God's Word and Spirit at work in him, creating a new beginning.

If we read but one side of Israel's story until Jesus, we could imagine that the prophet from Nazareth came out of thin air. But there was another story equally Jewish, poised in Israel's memory, ready to be brought to light.

Matthew and the Story of Light

To retrieve it, we need only read from Isaiah. Modern scholars have correctly divided Isaiah into three segments based upon the references of each to different time periods. The segments are chapters 1–39; 40–55; and 56–66. For the sake of clarity, they call them First Isaiah, Second Isaiah, and Third Isaiah. First Isaiah may include a few chapters from a later time period, but for our purposes, we may think broadly of three different historical contexts to which the chapters I have identified belong.

Whether or not Jesus or Matthew knew about the three divisions of Isaiah, I don't know. One major discovery at the Qumran community of

---

3. Wright, *New Testament*, 181, 185.
4. Theissen, *Early Palestinian Christianity*, 77.

the Essenes was a complete scroll of Isaiah in Hebrew, all sixty-six chapters intact. With that, the oldest scroll of Isaiah yet discovered, we may assume that Isaiah was thought to be one whole, and it was read as authored by a single prophet.

As we have noted, Matthew quotes Isaiah 9 in 4:12–16. "Galilee of the Gentiles—the people who sat in darkness have seen a great light, and for those who sat in the region and shadow of death light has dawned" (Matt 4:15–16).

A second reference by Matthew to Isaiah and light relates to the journey of the magi in chapter 2. Though not quoted explicitly, how could those who heard or read Matthew not think of Isaiah 60:1–3; 6: "Arise, shine; for your light has come, and the glory of the Lord has risen upon you. For darkness shall cover the earth and thick darkness the peoples; but the Lord will arise upon you, and his glory will appear over you. Nations [read Gentiles] shall come to your light, and kings to the brightness of your dawn . . A multitude of camels shall cover you, the young camels of Midian and Ephah; all those from Sheba shall come. They shall bring gold and frankincense, and shall proclaim the praise of the Lord."

Did Matthew make up the journey of the foreigners to Bethlehem? I don't know. Did he hear a story, perhaps from Mary herself, of some Gentile visitors at Jesus' birth and find credence for it in the Isaiah prophecy? I wonder. But what is clear is how Matthew relates light from Isaiah to the story of Jesus' arrival on the scene, both his birth and his ministry.

We have a reference from First Isaiah and Third Isaiah. The third reference to Isaiah and light echoes Second Isaiah. "I am the Lord, I have called you in righteousness, I have taken you by the hand and kept you; I have given you as a covenant to the people, a light to the nations, to open the eyes that are blind, to bring out the prisoners from the dungeon, from the prison those who sit in darkness. I am the Lord, that is my name; my glory I give to no other, nor my praise to idols. See, the former things have come to pass, and new things I now declare; before they spring forth, I tell you of them" (Isa 42:6–9).

If the words of Isaiah 42 sound familiar, they foreshadow what Jesus will tell John's disciples who had asked about him from prison, whether or not he is the one to come (Matt 11:2–6). The evangelist, like a great chef, marinates Jesus' response to John's disciples, not only in Isaiah 42, but also in Isaiah 29:18–19 and 35:5–6, two other passages where there is direct mention of the eyes of the blind that would see.

The great American composer Aaron Copland, who also scored ten movie soundtracks, once said that music for film was like "a lamp lit under the screen to warm it." Isaiah's theme of light underscores Matthew in that way. Isaiah 61:1–4 is another rich variation in sound: "The spirit of the Lord God is upon me, because the Lord has anointed me; he has sent me to bring good news to the oppressed, to bind up the brokenhearted, to proclaim liberty to the captives, and release to the prisoners; to proclaim the year of the Lord's favor . . . to comfort all who mourn; to provide for those who mourn in Zion—to give them a garland instead of ashes. . . . They will be called oaks of righteousness, the planting of the Lord to display his glory."

"The planting of the Lord to display his glory" should remind us that glory is kin to light. Holding onto the phrase "display God's glory or light," let's return to Second Isaiah 49:6: "It is too light a thing that you should be my servant to raise up the tribes of Jacob and to restore the survivors of Israel; I will give you as a light to the nations, that my salvation may reach to the end of the earth."

Jesus seems to develop these words in the Sermon on the Mount in Matthew. "You are the light of the world. A city set on a hill cannot be hid. No one after lighting a lamp puts it under a bushel basket, but on the lampstand, and it gives light to all in the house. In the same way, let your light shine before others, so that they may see your good works and give glory to your Father in heaven" (Matt 5:14–16). I suggest that this is more than an admonition to do good works. Rather, it is a commission to take up Israel's role as "light to the nations, that my salvation may reach to the end of the earth."

In Matthew, Jesus takes up Israel's prophetic role to serve as a light to the nations. From Isaiah to the Sermon on the Mount to the Great Commission, the mission is of bearing the light of God to the nations. According to Matthew, Jesus fulfills the role of Israel. Rather than narrowing the boundaries by hiding the light under a bushel basket, Jesus calls the people to be a renewed Israel to exhibit the light of God and God's salvation (God's work) to the world.

The Nature of God and the Mission of Light and Grace

In the words of the theologian of John's Gospel, "The light shines in the darkness, and the darkness did not overcome it" (John 1:5). As with John, so with Matthew, the purpose of the light is to reveal, not to conceal or to narrow. In other words, there is a directional purpose in the Gospels whether "I am the light of the world" (John 8:12) as Jesus says in John, or "God with Us" as Matthew calls Jesus. The message is from the person and work of God to the darkness.

This message informs how we should read the Gospels generally and Matthew in particular. As we read English from left to right and Hebrew from right to left, we should read in the way our texts invite us to read, not the reverse.

This speaks to my childhood fear of those passages which preachers sat upon, "The Son of Man will send his angels, and they will collect out of his kingdom all causes of sin and all evildoers, and they will throw them into the furnace of fire, where there will be weeping and gnashing of teeth" (Matt 13:41–42). Matthew seems to be strewn with such as these. Again, of the seven "weeping and gnashing" passages in the New Testament, six are in Matthew, and one in Luke, which is shared with Matthew.

It is true that Jesus uses the phrase "weeping and gnashing of teeth" to portray a place of torment. Five times the phrase occurs related to parables. Only once does it occur related to prose. But in every instance, the place of torment represents separation related to something a person or persons have done. Is such language to depict the nature of a vengeful deity, one who is out to get us?

Let's consider a passage that turns this view around. In Matthew 25, there is the parable of the talents. The parable appears in Luke with a similar form, but not the same emphasis as in Matthew.

"A man going on a journey called his servants and entrusted to them his property. To one he gave five talents, to another, two, and to another, one" (Matt 25:14–15). Then the man returns to see how each one has done with the amount he gave. It's a familiar parable. The one who was given five gained five more and was commended for it. The one given two gained two and was similarly commended. But where Luke gives roughly the same amount of space in storytelling to all three, Matthew expands on the person who received one talent (seven verses out of seventeen total). Why?

When the one-talent servant is asked why he buried the master's money, his response is curious. "I knew that you were a harsh man, reaping where you did not sow, and gathering where you did not scatter seed; so I was afraid" (Matt 25: 24). To emphasize in the parable the totally inaccurate perception of this servant, the master says, "You wicked and lazy slave! You knew, did you, that I reap where I did not sow, and gather where I did not scatter? Then you ought to have invested my money with the bankers, and on my return I would have received what was my own with interest" (Matt 25:26–27).

There is no indication in the parable that the master was anything but generous, not setting anyone up to fail. I used to think that he was unfair in taking the one talent away from the hiding servant to give it to those who already had more. But there is no indication in the parable that the master regarded this particular servant less than the other two. What does Jesus in Matthew stress?

Here's someone who did not know the master at all. In fact, the fearful servant presumed that the property owner was out to get him. If we want to read God in place of the master, the parable through the one-talent person's narrow perception introduces a kind of Kafkaesque deity. That is, we will be judged guilty for that which we have not been charged and of which we are unaware. Does the parable suggest behavior that results when we have no clue that God is gracious?

That is a serious misunderstanding of who God is. Such perception is as far wrong as hell is from heaven. Hence, "weeping and gnashing of teeth." Yet, some have wanted to move with the tortuous punishment imagery to project it back upon the deity. And I have found that hell, fire, and brimstone perceptions of God result, not in generous behaviors, loving and kind, but in those which turn the fires of hell up on their neighbors.

A similar but somewhat different parable is that of those hired to work in the vineyard. Cutting to the chase, those hired at the last hour of the workday are paid the same as those hired to work all day.

When there arises a protest by those who had suffered "the burden and heat of the day," the response by the vineyard owner is priceless. "Did you not agree to work for what I paid you? . . . Am I not allowed to do what I choose with what belongs to me? Or are you envious because I am generous? So the last will be first, and the first will be last" (Matt 20:13–16).

Again there is a misreading of generosity. In fact, there is no awareness of the master or vineyard owner being generous at all. Does this, perhaps, address persons in Matthew's congregation who are put out with the late-coming Gentiles who received the same grace as the longsuffering Jews? Those bedraggled ones who come late or last to the party may appreciate its fare more than those who have taken the spread for granted.

After many years teaching the parable of the prodigal son (in Luke, not Matthew), I began to be aware that more people sympathized with the elder brother than the younger son. Sounding like the father speaking to his older son, an old translation of Matthew 20:15 has it, "Do you begrudge my generosity?"

Synonyms for "begrudge" are "envy" and "resent." The *New Revised Standard Version* translates verse 15, "Are you envious because I am generous?" But that old word "begrudge" has a sound that fits what it is, like someone who is grumbling and grinding her teeth while choking back something. God's grace and generosity are more often met with resentment than we may realize. We appreciate them in theory as long as God's attentions are directed to people we basically like. But when they never volunteer to set up for coffee, prepare communion for Christmas Eve, or come to clean-up day with their brooms and rakes, we can be resentful. Occasionally the church likes to write the rules for how God is to act rather than celebrate with joy what God has to give.

Perhaps we had rather God give 'em hell than learn to sit at the same table, sharing the gifts of bread and wine. Grace like light has a direction that we cannot reverse even when those old preachers wanted to pound on phrases like "weeping and gnashing of teeth."

Hope and Grapple

When the story of our faith loses touch with the vision of a bountiful God, human identity can be constricted and the boundaries of our living can become narrow. Jesus in Matthew moves from gracious Beatitudes to the creation of a new people, beginning with those most in need of help (Matt 5). Jesus in Matthew feels deep, gut-level compassion toward all those tormented with disease and demons, who are lost like sheep without a shepherd. And he prays the Lord of the harvest for more workers to be about the signs of the kingdom (Matt 9). Jesus in Matthew expands the bounds of forgiveness from a generous seven times to an extraordinary, almost unbelievable, seventy times seven (Matt 18). How wide is God's mercy!

That is the story of God with Us. But whether in the church today or the world around us, I share the concern of Charles Taylor that we may be losing touch with the story if we have not already lost our way home.

I sat with a clergyman who had taken part in leading the memorial service for Matthew Shephard. Shephard was a gay man, a student at the University of Wyoming, who was beaten, tortured, tied to a fence post, and left to die on October 6, 1998. As the worship leaders processed to the Episcopal Cathedral in Denver, they passed through a gauntlet of protesters with ugly voices and hateful placards. These were Christians who decried homosexuality as sin according to their view of Scripture. It did not seem to matter to them how Matthew Shephard had been treated, only that he had violated God's law.

As I sat with the preacher at Shephard's memorial service some months afterward, he was still reeling with reaction to those protesters. To someone who had grown up with more conservative Christians than he, his plea was, "Help me understand them."

In fairness, most conservative Christians I have known (that is, those who regard homosexuality as a sin according to scripture and church teaching) would deplore the violence done to Shephard and any verbiage akin to it. But there was an evil tone against persons of God's creation in the voices and on the placards of protesters outside the cathedral in Denver that day.

Many people are embarrassed to have anything to do with a god who would sanction such a tone. No doubt, some have fled the story of faith for reasons such as that.

I am reminded of a similar flight from the story by two former confirmands who did not want me to marry them because they no longer saw themselves as Christians. The reason they gave was a conflict between science and faith in God. I was disturbed by this because I presumed I had done an adequate job of showing that there need be no opposition between the pursuits of science and the steps of belief. Nonetheless, the struggle is real.

My own history has led me to believe that faith in God has suffered due to the reduction of all knowledge to what can be proven by the five senses. On the religious side, God has been argued as if the result of a syllogism without a deep sense of mystery. On the science and philosophy side, faith has been scorned because it cannot be determined by empirical evidence. This, in effect, denies the reality of such things as beauty, creation's goodness, a human being's worth, justice, love, suffering, and truth, which we assume functionally but whose reality we cannot prove.

As Taylor observes, "We are all universalists now about respect for life and integrity . . . [which means] that we believe it would be utterly wrong and unfounded to draw the boundaries any narrower than around the whole human race."[5] By "we are all" Taylor is referring to the cohort of humanistically-oriented academics and intellectuals. I admit they are people like some of my best friends, compassionate and generous spirits.

But many of the same crowd have undercut belief in God and reliance on the biblical story of God as without substance. The question must be raised: On what do we base our universal values? On what do we base our assumption that the best views and practices of a tall humanity really apply to others than our particular tribe? And in an era when tribalism seems on the rise, and world problems are more complicated, what moral and spiritual resources are there for welcoming more to the table than those like the intimate group to which we personally belong? Encountering and welcoming the totally other (even the strange, new world of retirement) is like a death to something. Wherein do we find strength to die on the way to life?

---

5. Taylor, *Sources of the Self*, 6–7.

CHAPTER FOURTEEN

Wide and Deep

IN A WORLD IN which narrow religious views are packaged in the form of terrorist attacks, many people have raised questions about exclusive confessional beliefs. Regular churchgoers are no exception to this line of questioning. In fact, "I am the way, the truth and the life" (John 14:6) has been as troubling in adult Bible classes as anywhere, probably because those folk are still capable of quoting a few verses of Scripture. But let's table John 14:6 for now to ask, "What does Matthew say about Jesus' role in God's salvation?"

We turn to Matthew 12:9–14. After Jesus had healed a man with a withered hand on the Sabbath, this so offended the Pharisees that they conspired how they might destroy him. As we follow the narrative closely, Jesus, knowing what they were up to, moves away from them, but, as usual, a great crowd stays with him. He continues to heal them all, but he tells them not to make him known (Matt 12:15–16).

Scholars have called attention to passages in the Gospels that seem awkwardly patched together and so do not seem to fit together. That can be an accurate reading, depending on the particular text. What it can ignore, however, is the author's narrative logic. In other words, what is Matthew saying to us about Jesus in the very way that he leads us through the story?

The Pharisees represent for Matthew a narrow, overly strict understanding of Israel's identity and purpose. In chapter 12, this viewpoint is woven into a net to entangle Jesus. For the time being, Jesus escapes. Not being stupid, he does not want to be caught before his work is complete. It makes sense that he sternly cautions the crowd not to uncork the wine before it is time. In this reticence to call attention to himself, Matthew sees an echo of Isaiah.

"Here is my servant, whom I have chosen, my beloved, with whom my soul is well pleased. I will put my Spirit upon him, and he will proclaim justice to the Gentiles. He will not wrangle or cry aloud, nor will anyone hear his voice in the streets. He will not break a bruised reed or quench a smoldering wick until he brings justice to victory. And in his name the Gentiles will hope" (Matt 12:18–21; Isa 42:1–4, quoted the Seputagint, the Greek version of the Old Testament).[1]

The servant of Isaiah in whom Matthew sees Jesus was not one to call attention to himself. He did not use a bullhorn. Rarely was he a bull in a china closet. He wasn't a windbag, full of himself, sucking all the air out of the room. Rather, he went about his work cautiously and deliberately so as to pursue the mission to its ultimate conclusion.

What was it? Matthew and the Septuagint say it clearly, "that in him the Gentiles will hope." This fits with everything that Matthew has drawn forward from Isaiah. It finds coherence in the whole of Matthew's story from the Gentile magi coming to the light of Israel in Bethlehem to the Risen Christ sending the disciples to teach all the Gentiles.

In this most Jewish of the Gospels, who is Jesus but the one who fulfills the servant role in Isaiah to take the light revealed to Israel to the end of the earth (Is. 49:6)? But "Will the Jews be saved?" some Christians have asked. I am not sure that Matthew would even understand the question. It imports such extra baggage for traveling with Matthew.

As our passage strongly indicates, the tension that Jesus surfaces is within Judaism itself. It is between two old views of Israel's identity and purpose.

We only need to think of Jonah in the Old Testament. Whether or not a person could survive in the belly of a great fish is quite beside the point. Actually Jonah may have been a subversive story to those who were rallying the troops around a narrow identity of Jewish life which they felt was threatened by assimilation.

The Old Testament scholar and biblical theologian Bernhard Anderson sharpens the point well: "At the very time when the politics of Ezra and Nehemiah were fostering a narrow nationalism and a doctrinaire exclusivism, the unknown prophet of the book of Jonah proclaimed 'the mystery of God's compassion' (Abraham Heschel, *The Prophets*). Yahweh's grace cannot be programmed theologically or circumscribed by exclusive boundaries, for Yahweh is free to 'be gracious unto whom I will be gracious' and 'to show mercy upon whom I will show mercy' (Exodus 33:19)."[2]

---

1. Rahlfs and Hanhart, *Septuaginta*.
2. Anderson, *Understanding*, 607.

The passion of Jesus for the gospel of God's kingdom extended as wide as God's creation. In Matthew and the other Gospels, we see how it conflicts with a narrow view of Israel. What was at stake is no less than how far the light of revelation would shine. Would it be limited to a certain set of Jews? Or, would it pursue the vision of Isaiah and Jonah?

What I am taking pains to show is that this was an old argument the beginnings of which may be traced to hundreds of years before Jesus. Also, it was an argument within Judaism itself. Or, as some advise, it might be better to speak of Judaisms. What became Christianity and mostly Gentile was originally a Jewish vision of God's purposes for all creation. Jesus was simply taking it on the road.

As to the question, "Will the Jews be saved?" I imagine that Matthew would have a similar view to Paul. "The gifts and calling of God (to Israel) are irrevocable" (Romans 11:29). The question that exercises Matthew is, "Will the Gentiles take part?" In Jesus was their hope. Without Jesus there was no turning to the Gentile world. Without Jesus, we the Gentiles would remain in darkness just as did "Galilee of the Gentiles" (Matt 4:15–16) before the light of Christmas dawned upon them. Its point of origin in Matthew was when "Jesus began to proclaim, 'repent, for the kingdom of heaven has come near'" (Matt 4:17).

Comments Around the Edges

As I write, I am well aware of how conversation goes when we put the spotlight on Jesus. Rather than the Pharisees or some others, Jesus himself and/or those who told his story in the New Testament are thought to be exclusive.

"Everyone . . . who acknowledges me before others, I also will acknowledge before my Father in heaven; but whoever denies me before others, I also will deny before my Father in heaven" (Matt 10:32–33). "Woe to you Bethsaida! For if the deeds of power done in you had been done in Tyre and Sidon, they would have repented long ago in sackcloth and ashes. But I tell you, on the day of judgment it will be more tolerable for Tyre and Sidon than for you" (Matt 11: 21–22).

Compare the tone of those words with these of Jeremiah. "How can you say, 'We are wise, and the law of the Lord is with us,' when, in fact, the false pen of the scribes has made it into a lie? The wise shall be put to shame, they shall be dismayed and taken; since they have rejected the word of the Lord, what wisdom is in them?" (Jer 8:8–9).

In Scripture, prophets, including Jesus, don't mince words. They don't speak in both/ands, continuums, or nuances. They provide clear paths of difference, roads that greatly diverge, to reference Frost.

Consider also, "Truly I tell you, in no one in Israel have I found such faith [Jesus says to the Gentile centurion]. I tell you, many will come from east and west and will eat with Abraham, Isaac, and Jacob in the kingdom of heaven, while the heirs of the kingdom will be thrown into outer darkness" (Matt 8: 10–11).

For those worried that Jesus is speaking against Jews per se, there are three of the greatest, Abraham, Isaac, and Jacob, already dining in the kingdom of heaven. What Jesus evokes is the problem with heirs. It is the same problem that John the Baptist had in Matthew 3, "Do not presume to say to yourselves, 'We have Abraham as our ancestor'; for I tell you, God is able from these stones to raise up children to Abraham" (Matt 3:9). At issue is whether responding to the covenant God in faith or trotting out one's DNA marks a true child of the kingdom.

Also, who has not heard some people say, "All religions are like different paths to the same god. They all teach pretty much the same thing. One religion is just as good as another"? I imagine them grumbling as they come away from the front door where they've just been asked if they know Jesus Christ as their personal savior. Is it not possible that a course correction might benefit both door knockers and those who wish they hadn't opened it?

No question, Matthew, like the rest of the New Testament, engages in the scandal of particularity. Jesus is the light who reveals God; no one else occupies that unique position. To my mind, that does not deny angles of religious vision to persons outside Christian faith. Neither does it consign all such persons to hell but those who accept Jesus Christ as their Lord and Savior.

It is interesting to me that those who have the right words are not necessarily on the threshold of the kingdom. "Not everyone who says to me, 'Lord, Lord,' will enter the kingdom of heaven, but only the one who does the will of my Father in heaven" (Matt 7:21). This is similar to those in the great judgment parable who are commended for feeding the hungry, welcoming the stranger, clothing the naked, caring for the sick and visiting those in prison. They were not aware that they had done anything religious, that is, that they had actually been attending to the Son of Man when they cared for the least (Matt 25:31–40).

The more I have thought about Christ's mercy and my need for it, the less I have been inclined to sort out the saved and the damned. And the deeper we dive into this story of the self-giving God, the wider God's arms seem to extend to embrace all creation.

Jesus once told a parable, saying, "The kingdom of heaven may be compared to someone who sowed good seed in his field; but while everybody was asleep, an enemy came and sowed weeds among the wheat, and then went away. So when the plants came up and bore grain, then the weeds appeared as well." The servants then wanted to know if the master wanted them to go to work on removing the weeds. But this reply speaks loudly, "No; for in gathering the weeds you would uproot the wheat along with them. Let both of them grow together until the harvest," then he will tell the reapers what to do (Matt 13: 24–30).

But why not postulate a deity who is a kind of amalgamation of the best gods and ideas about religion? This would serve the purpose of sidestepping all those knotty passages with their sharp differences and severe punishment. This meta-deity seems rather popular these days, a kind of imaginary or theoretical figure quite beyond human foibles and the ouchiness of historical persons who muck around with the likes of us.

Related to this above-all deity, there is a pantheistic view of god as all and everything. "Each of us is god and god is each of us" puts it close to what one church member told me. In this view, there is no distinction between a transcendent deity and earthly, physical existence (God over against creation), for everything is equally part and parcel of the same reality whether gods, angels, humans, demons, sticks, stones, or dirt. As I hear it, there is not necessarily a separate focus upon any god in this view, whether in heaven or on earth, but a great indistinguishable oneness. Whether for good or ill, this is simply not a view that inhabits the Bible, Hebrew or Christian.

This is also a deity without a story, hence a deity without an identity. A meta-deity, detextualized, is quite beyond anything that we can know. Though Scripture tells us (Phil 4:6) that God surpasses knowledge, that is, surpasses what we can know and control, we are yet given assurance that the peace of God will guard our hearts and minds in Christ Jesus (the story).

Not to put too fine a point on it, how do we know whether or not the god beyond all religions is good or bad, for us or against us, a personal being or a cosmic force field? When I feel harassed and haunted by my inmost thoughts, when I feel guilty and ground down on paths that I have taken, when I feel anxious and despairing about an unknown future, does a deity without a story travel with me or leave me alone like some far away galaxy?

At the same time, I am not unsympathetic towards those who struggle to sort out Jesus in Matthew. He does have that prophetic edge that cuts to my hypersensitivity. But when my exaggerated confidence and my overweening sensitivity have been laid bare by this story, I glimpse light and grace. Once again, "Come unto me all you that are weary and carrying burdens, and I will give you rest" (Matt 11: 28).

Artists, Mystics, Poets and Such

The Thirty Years' War on the continent of Europe lasted from 1618 to 1648. It was ostensibly a conflict between Roman Catholics and Protestants. More than likely it was a conflict between the different agendas of those who controlled the lands mostly populated by Roman Catholics and Protestants.

When it was all done, six and a half million lay dead, strewn across a weary landscape. There is not much evidence that this massive strife resulted in anything but deep pessimism concerning religious belief. Some see in the Thirty Years' War more than the corpses of a military conflict. They read into it liberation from those old cadavers, religion and ancient philosophy, that weighed upon the pursuit of knowledge.

Yet, when there are seismic shifts from one era to another, sometimes those with special sight offer the best insight. The clergyman-poet George Herbert was one such person. At some time during the Thirty Years War on the continent, he penned this verse in England, a kind of commentary on John 14: 6:

> Come, my way, my truth, my life;
> Such a way as gives us breath
> Such a truth as ends all strife
> Such a life as killeth death.[3]

Given a background of rather exclusive Christianity, when I read "Such a way as gives us breath," it almost took my breath away. This was not my way or the highway. It was a way that took us beyond landscapes scattered and weary with death. It was a way that took us through death itself and every hold death has on us to life beyond measure. "Such a way as gives us breath."

Hope and Grapple

Let's continue with Herbert's commentary that the way of Christ is "such a way as gives us breath." It is not a far leap to God with Us. As a theme in Matthew, God with Us surrounds and abides the whole Gospel. It occurs at the dawn of Jesus' birth, at midday in a church conflict, and toward

---

3. Herbert, *Country Parson and the Temple*, 249–250.

the horizon as we lose hold of time. Where life challenges to randomize, to polarize, and to obliterate meaning with chaos, God with Us is the Sacred Between that gathers, embraces and enlightens.

In Matthew 18, Christ is in the midst of a community, striving to reconcile the one who has somehow turned against it. As anyone knows who has dealt with conflicts and misbehaviors that threaten the body of Christ, this work is among the most challenging and least rewarding we face.

I am thinking of a letter that was on my desk when I arrived at one congregation. It spoke of a pedophile who had done damage for years. I checked out the facts, followed our Child Safety Protection Policy and with an elder spoke to this individual with our expectations. At least one person thought we were being unchristian in our approach. But we had to protect our children and the reputation of the congregation.

The words of Jesus are most welcome at such times. "Where two or three are gathered in my name, there I am in your midst." When ministry is not pretty but necessary and graciousness is not much felt, we need the Sacred Between to hold us and get us through.

The Sacred Between of Christ's presence occurs where forgiveness may be hard and getting lost may be easy. I take it that Jesus gives the church the authority to bind and to loose, not as some institutional means of playing god, but as a common place on earth where God's presence in the midst of human anguish and confusion may be known.

To other possibilities, God is with us across our years. When decades have passed and body and mind are failing, a wilderness can loom. Who am I now that I have no position? Who am I now that my parents are gone and my friends are passing? Who am I now that no one remembers where I came from, what my achievements and struggles have been, what joys and sorrows I have known?

In 2011 I attended a gathering at Iona Abbey. There I met Murdoch and Anne MacKenzie, who were members of the Iona community and leaders for the week. We shared many stories.

Among them was that I had traveled on an evangelistic mission to South India more than forty years prior. During that time, my partner in mission and I slid to the pavement from our motorcycle, greased by a pile of cow dung. Wearing flip flops because we had to cross a stream and no helmet, I both shaved skin from the side of my foot and cracked my head to unconsciousness on the asphalt road.

Our means for getting back to town and the rustic hotel was an ox cart that the local folk stopped for us. My friend was a high school football star and so recognized my upchucking as the sign of a concussion. As he was kneeling in prayer in the corner of my room, a Lutheran pastor, whom we had previously met, appeared at the door. Together they went down to the street and hailed an ambulance. It was returning patients from Dr. Beard's Methodist Mission Hospital. There I stayed in her gracious care for about four days until my foot was better and my headaches had subsided.

Coincidentally Murdoch and Anne had been missionaries in South India, where he was ordained as pastor and she served as a medical doctor. They knew Dr. Beard from their time there.

Next day Murdoch asked if he might speak to me before our session began. He had a woven cloth bag in hand. It so happened that when they had been on furlough in North India, they were trying to locate their train from the overhead announcement boards in Delhi. Not knowing Hindi, the language of the north, they were struggling to find the right train when a man approached them, asking if they were Christians.

Christians are by far the minority in India, so they were curious. The man had recognized the bag they carried which was crafted by patients at Dr. Beard's hospital. Hearing my story, Murdoch and Anne wanted me to have it which was the purpose of that brief gifting moment So, I now have this treasure in earthen colors.

In ways I cannot explain, a simple cloth hand bag symbolizes the Sacred Between of my life's years. From Chennai to Iona, my time here seems more than days randomly strung together. Another hand, like a great seamstress, has taken care with them. I believe there are vantage points for looking back at providence and giving thanks.

More specific to Matthew 18, a crowd becomes community by the Sacred Between. Yet, between our troubling differences, separated by silos of uniqueness or worn down by cycles of familiarity, we can become mere problems to one another.

Often in counseling those to be married, I have drawn on my own experience, saying that we should continue to receive one another as a gift. And the gift of a person is akin to the gift of beauty. In Udaipur, India, I woke about 2 AM to light pouring through the curtains of our hotel window. Quietly I rose, not waking Joanna, and parted the sheer curtains just behind heavy drapes. A full moon had risen over the mountains in the distance and was casting a sparkling path of light across the lake.

The whole scene was visually extraordinary and took me out of myself. I had no idea that night how many others were arrested by such beauty. It had made its way to our room, and I felt its light shone for me. The next day, I couldn't adequately describe it.

Another person in marriage, in friendship, in serendipity is a gift to receive. Through long years of marriage, he or she is like the moon over Udaipur if we but have eyes and heart to see. But how can there be such bountiful togetherness if there is no thanksgiving for what captures our attention and uplifts us? Is it not the Sacred Between that makes us more than a crowd, an anonymous mass, a pretzel of flesh, the press of one will upon another?

Now, let's round out this grappling with similar vignettes about receiving gifts. The Sacred Between awakens us to Scripture as more than mere words on the pages of the Bible. The likes of Karl Barth and Martin Buber speak with reverence of the old Hebrew and Christian texts as a meeting place with God. The book as we hold it in our hands is not God. But it is unique as entre to the story of God with Us. When we pray the Holy Spirit for illumination, we are not asking that we be lit up. We are, rather, requesting eyes to see and believe our way through the passages and passageways of the story, God coming to be among us, even today.

It is my belief that once we find ourselves put together by the Sacred Between, the whole of life is more available. More than glops on canvas, there is a Renoir gallery of color. More than a cacophony of noise, it is an *Ode to Joy*, Beethoven's *Ninth*. More than a seemingly random placement of food and decoration, it is a welcome home and warm embrace at Thanksgiving. Life can pass us by, boring and flat, unless grace and gratitude halt us in our tracks. Life can be robbed of everything exquisite, meaningful, inspirational by the dullness of our spirits.

The Sacred Between restores life to its proper dimension when it has been distorted and oppressed. And even when it has been brutalized and suffocated, there is a divine presence that abides suffering and gives us once again room for hoping and believing. "Such a way as gives us breath."

CHAPTER FIFTEEN

Lost in Matthew, Chaos and Hope

IN THE AFTERMATH OF a bombing attack, the scene of chaos, including mangled victims, appears on our screens. The voices sent to report often say something about senseless suffering or senseless violence. No doubt, television crews are caught up in the emotion, trying to portray with their pictures what words cannot express. I truly appreciate the reserve in most of their commentaries. "Senseless suffering or violence" is about right.

In my opinion, faith talk should partake of the same reserve. When the attack on the World Trade Towers in New York City took place, I was living and serving as a pastor in a mile-square village in a densely populated county of Long Island. Like all the villages and counties around the City, numerous commuters made their way to Manhattan every day. Also, our village was like so many others in the metropolitan area, where firefighters and police officers lived but worked at fire stations and precincts across the rivers. In those first hours and even days, the whereabouts of so many of our own was unknown.

I was the convener of the local clergy group at that time. Suddenly on the streets, I ceased to be pastor of the Community Presbyterian Church and became pastor of the whole community. Others did too. With a few phone calls, we put together a prayer service two days after the attack in the auditorium of the middle school. A shattered people gathered, looking to God for comfort and hope.

The service leaders were people from our churches and the Jewish Center. We had religious diversity from Catholic, Jewish, and Protestant communities, and we came together in heart and mind. We learned eventually that four persons from our village had died in ways related to 9/11. But that evening, we did not know about them and others. The atmosphere was palpably anxious.

And yet one community of faith took their time on the religious stage to "thank God and praise the Lord." I was dumbstruck and deeply offended. Not at all because I do not believe in either thanking God or praising the Lord and vigorously, but we were there not knowing whether our relatives and friends were dead or alive. *Faith needs to be with others differently in the midst of chaos when announcements of loss are pending.*

As promised, I must offer my own struggles on this journey with Matthew, grappling with hope. As I have read over and over passages such as those in Matthew chapters 10 and 24 referring to the end, I have gotten lost. To put it succinctly, traveling with Matthew, I have gotten lost in Matthew.

The passages are challenging even to the academic community, those with the greatest skills as exegetes, textual critics, and historical scholars. What sense can be made of the words and sentences themselves and to what do they refer?

As a preacher and pastor, having gone through chaos with one community, I read Matthew as a preacher and pastor, seeking to guide a people through chaos. His work was to bring forward the message of Jesus and teaching about Jesus to comfort those who had suffered the Jewish war with the Romans that took place between 66 and 73 CE of the first century.

I am not saying that the persons who read Matthew were necessarily at ground zero of that conflict. But as we were deeply affected in the suburbs of New York City, even with loss of life, I am suggesting that Matthew and the Jesus followers he attended to were also deeply affected. My argument is simply that the language of Matthew reflects the chaos that people endured. With this in mind, let's attempt to inhabit that language and what we can know of the conflict to which Jesus in Matthew refers.

Reading What is Before Us with Our Mind's Eye

Just as enduring the attacks of 9/11 in proximity to Ground Zero at the World Trade Towers afforded a different perspective than following the horror from across the country, so it is with Matthew. But the best we can do to retrieve the immediate context of the Gospel writer is to follow the historians. Josephus, the ancient Jewish Roman general and historian of both *The Antiquities of the Jews* and *The Jewish War*, offers much story and detail of those times. But I am following a highly-regarded 19th-century German historian by the name of Emil Schurer, who has done his homework with

Josephus but is also aware of that author's tendency to flatter himself in telling his tale.[1]

I offer only a few salient features of the Jewish War with the Romans which lasted from 66 CE in Galilee to the astonishment and horror at Masada in 73 CE. For persons like me who have known somewhat about the destruction of Jerusalem in 70 CE and its significance for both Jews and Jewish Christians, I must round out the picture.

First, the scope of the conflict was greater than I had imagined. More than a five month siege of Jerusalem from April 14, just before Passover, to September 8, when the city finally fell to the Romans, the war took place all over Palestine.

Second, it was indeed a war. Vespasian, the Roman general, amassed an army of 60,000 soldiers to encompass the Jewish held lands. The number of Jewish freedom fighters whom Josephus calls "zealots" must have been considerable, because they managed to go toe to toe with the battle-savvy Roman legions. The Romans were stunned by the passion, fury, and wiliness with which the Jews fought.

Third, not all Jews were of the same mind when it came to the Roman occupation. Schurer categorizes as "aristocrats" an uneasy alliance of Jewish puppet royalty like the Agrippas, the chief priests in charge of the temple, and the Pharisees who wanted to protect the temple and its religious functions. This segment of society Schurer calls the "Party of Order." As for the common people, some may have sided with the Party of Order, but they were of a range of opinion that varied in their attitudes toward Rome. And we should not overlook the fact that loyalties fluctuated.

Fourth, those Jews who had had enough of Roman rule organized a rebellion that lined up behind a variety of leaders who did not always keep their opposition united. In fact, two of the most charismatic and power hungry leaders, John of Gischala and Simon Bar-Giora, while ensconced in Jerusalem, engaged one another with their troops in bloody street fighting. Those who got in their way suffered as if they were the enemy itself. Only when Titus' army was knocking at the gates, actually employing battering rams, moveable ramparts, and siege ramps, did John and Simon sacrifice their egos to join forces, but by then it was too late.

Fifth, Josephus himself took part in the rebellion as a young man of about thirty and was captured but managed to escape by stealth. Suggesting that his fellow-captives should fall upon one another with their swords rather than submit to Roman crosses, Josephus ended up as the lone survivor and walked out to surrender. By playing the part of a prophet, he predicted

---

1. Schurer, *Jewish People*, Section 20.

his rise to the rank of general in the Roman army, which did, in fact, happen, and ingratiated himself to his captors. His story indicates how loyalties were not always fixed, and survival could depend on being clever enough to shift with the winds of power.

Sixth, everywhere both Jewish and Roman fighters went, they left death and destruction in their wake. Those who suffered were not only those vested in the various militias but women, children, shopkeepers, and anyone unfortunate enough not to flee the rampage of violence. Many Jews were crucified, such as those trying to escape Jerusalem in search of food. Titus fixed the caught onto crosses staked on the hills round about to discourage the remaining defenders. As indicated, famine led to demise for those under siege in the holy city. Previously and thoughtlessly, John and Simon in their intramural combat inside Jerusalem had destroyed granaries which could have nourished and extended the battle.

It is my opinion that the language of Matthew about the days to come and the end reflects in apocalyptic imagery the actual horror of the Jewish war with Rome. Though a number of Jewish Christians fled Jerusalem before the last days, they would have well known what was taking place there. Jews all over Palestine would have heard reports of the worst from those who fled in desperation.

Jesus in Matthew gives warnings to pregnant women and those nursing infants to "pray that their flight not be in winter nor on a Sabbath" (Matt 24:19–20). Today, knowing a bit of the history, we do not have to stretch our imaginations to read actual situations of terror in those words.

We also read in Matthew 10 Jesus' disturbing words, "Think not that I came to bring peace on the earth but a sword. For I came to divide a man against his father and a daughter against her mother, and a bride against her mother-in-law, and the enemies of a man will be those of his own household" (Matt 10:34–36). A lesson of first-century history is that loyalties were torn.

Matthew contextualizes Jesus' words to exhort commitment to him. "Whoever does not take up his cross and follow after me is not worthy of me. Whoever finds his life will lose it, and she who loses her life for my sake will find it" (Matt 10:38–39, my translation). As with Bonhoeffer and the story of his theological and personal commitment in Nazi Germany, so here, the landscape of Palestine for the early Jewish Christians was not one of peace and calm but a journey threatened by the sword and the cross. Given all we know of Jesus, his was a mission of peace, but as Matthew reflects on his words and deeds for a later time, it was a peace hard won.

From "How a Poem Means" to "How a Gospel Means"

It is easy to get lost in Matthew if we must impose our own criteria of meaning upon the first Gospel. That is why it is so important to ask, "How does Matthew say what he wants to say?" Like travel to any part of the world where the culture is not familiar, there are points of contact, for sure, but to learn, we must stay open to seeing the world through a different lens.

As we have noted, Matthew 24 finds Jesus speaking about the end. The end of what? And why does he speak of the end in four different ways (24:3–14; 15–28; 29–31; and 32–35) before he gets to the end that no one knows (24:36)? As an aspect of our traveling with Matthew, I suggest that we set aside trying to pin him to a timeline.

Rather, the evangelist is like an impressionist painter and is presenting three or four different vignettes related to cataclysmic events. He is not painting realistically, as did Meindert Hobbema or another of the Dutch landscape artists who practically rendered every leaf on the tree. Nor is he photographing events such that we see exactly what an eyewitness might have seen. What technique, then, is he using, so that we may see what he wants us to?

I suggest that he is painting with the palette of the Old Testament in one hand and with his brush in the other, composing variations on the theme of the Son of Man taken largely from Daniel. On the anonymous Matthew's literary canvas, the Son of Man comes to life in the ministry, teaching, death, and resurrection of Jesus of Nazareth.

But to acknowledge that we have an artist at work in telling this story is not to say that the artist has fictionalized his subject out of thin air. Jesus is Matthew's inspiration. The outlines of Jesus' life are here just as we can see Rouen Cathedral in the series of paintings by Claude Monet. Or, perhaps a better example would be that of an artist who works in mosaics. A hundred tiles viewed separately might not make sense until together they depict the face of Christ. It is that holistic, coherent work that Matthew brings to light.

Let's look closer at the Son of Man in Matthew as drawn from Daniel. According to Daniel 7, in the prophet's night visions, he "saw one like a human being [others translate Son of Man] coming with the clouds of heaven. And he came to the Ancient One and was presented before him. To him was given dominion and glory and kingship, that all peoples, nations, and languages should serve him. His dominion is an everlasting dominion that shall not pass away, and his kingship is one that shall never be destroyed" (Dan 7:13–14). Matthew 24:30 seems to draw directly from this passage. "Then the sign of the Son of Man will appear in heaven, and then all the tribes of the earth will mourn, and they will see 'the Son of Man coming on the clouds of heaven' with power and great glory."

The words of Allison and Davies make sense to me as to what Matthew is doing with the reference to Daniel: "Pious Jews, hearing Daniel 7 read, and finding themselves persecuted or in a situation of suffering, would no doubt have viewed the events involving the one like a son of man as a promise of passage through affliction to victory: if Daniel's figure had suffered difficulty only to be given the triumph, so too the listeners might hope, might they be delivered from a painful predicament into the state of salvation."[2]

Again, according to Allison and Davies, "the phrase Son of Man appears thirty times (in Matthew), thirteen with reference to the future coming of the Son of Man, ten with reference to his death and resurrection, seven with reference to his earthly activity . . . The title seems to be used primarily of Jesus not in his relationship to God or to believers alone or to unbelievers alone but the world at large. This is why in the First Gospel the Son of Man is the eschatological judge (13:41; 19:28; 24:30,39; 25:31); why he will come publicly and be seen by all (10:23; 24: 27, 30; 25:31; 26:64); why Jesus answers enemies and outsiders by referring to himself as the Son of Man (11:19; 12:32,40; 26:24,64); why it is as the Son of Man that Jesus suffers at the hands of others; and why the ransom for many is paid by Jesus as the Son of Man."[3] (Matt 20:28)

Though Matthew employs imagery from Daniel to cast Jesus as the Son of Man, he does not view the situation of Israel as does Daniel. Daniel prays God to forgive the people of their sins for which they are suffering the current punishment (Dan 9). But Matthew views Jesus as the people's savior (Matt 1:21) and redeemer (Matt 20:28). He does what they, by repentance alone, cannot do for themselves. This is the reason that Matthew uses "Son of Man" in ten references to his death and resurrection; two particularly refer to his suffering before being killed (Matt 16:21; 20:19).

The Son of Man is God's person who comes in the midst of the people's suffering as a sign of compassion and hope. On the way to life, the Son of Man suffers in offering his life as God's ultimate sacrifice for the people. This same Son of Man is judge of the world, the one who died for the world and was raised as light and life for all people.

Matthew likens him to the suffering servant of Second Isaiah "in whose name the Gentiles will hope" (Matt 12:21; Isa 42:1–4, in the Septuagint) [4] I cannot help but see in Matthew the changed view of the people from First

---

2. Davies and Allison, *Matthew,* Vol. II, 50.
3. Davies and Allison, *Matthew,* Vol. II, 50–51.
4. Rahlfs and Hanhart, *Septuaginta.*

Isaiah and Daniel 9 to Second Isaiah. "Comfort, O comfort my people, says your God. Speak tenderly to Jerusalem, and cry to her that she has served her term, that her penalty is paid, that she has received from the Lord's hand double for all her sins" (Isa 40:1–2).

In his reference to the deportation to Babylon in the genealogy (Matt 1:11–12), Matthew hints that the time of the Christ is a time when the people are still in exile.[5] They still need saving from their sins.

But the situation has changed. It is no longer only sin, punishment, and pardon. It is chaos, despair, and meaninglessness. The kind of savior that is needed is different from a Maccabean-style redeemer or a John of Gischala / Simon Bar-Giora liberator. It is one who would bear the sins of the people on his shoulders as God with Us.

The Old Testament scholar and theologian Bernhard Anderson summarizes the change from First Isaiah and Daniel 9 to Second Isaiah and, I suggest, Matthew. "Yahweh's message is one of pardon and grace. Israel's past has been forgiven, not because sin and punishment have been balanced on the divine books, but only because the free gift of God's forgiveness makes a wholly new beginning (Isa 43:23; Jer 31:34), Israel stands on the threshold of the new age. The decisive moment has come. The time is fulfilled and the kingdom of God is drawing near."[6]

In a time of intense suffering where chaos interrupts history, "What have we done wrong?" pales in significance. It is not that we have not done wrong. Rather, that the weight of suffering has become unbearable to such an extent that we cannot lift it.

There were those at the time of 9/11 who said that the United States deserved this punishment for sins of homosexuality while others saw the attacks as punishment for U.S. greed and abuse of power as a nation. But nothing that anyone, individual or nation, had done wrong (presumed or real) deserved the horror of such suffering, death, and destruction.

"All we like sheep have gone astray; we have all turned to our own way, and the Lord has laid on him the iniquity of us all" (Isa 53: 6). Though not quoted directly in Matthew, Isaiah and Second Isaiah in particular are in reference. Close enough, verse 8:17 is a direct quote of Isaiah 53:4: "he has taken on our weaknesses and borne our diseases" (Matt 8:17). It is with the brush and paint of the suffering servant, the son of man, the Christ, Son of God, and God with Us that Matthew shows us the way through chaos, despair, and meaninglessness. This is the way of God with Us through death to life.

---

5. Wright, *New Testament*, 242, 299.
6. Anderson, *Understanding*, 477.

Hope and Grapple

For many years I stared at apocalyptic texts like Matthew 24 as the Christian Year began. This year again, Matthew 24:36–44 haunts the lectionary with this admonition. "You should be prepared, because the hour of the Son of Man will come when you do not expect" (Matt 24:44). What is this preparation for an unexpected hour? How can we watch for a time we cannot know? How do we live with a sense of the coming of God?

Once on a September night in Texas, I was watching the Miss America Pageant with my parents. The door of our den was open to the back porch because the evening was warm. Suddenly we could see light bright as day filling the back yard. It shone with an eerie resemblance to a storm's lightning, but there ensued neither rain nor wind. And it lasted for several seconds, longer than any flash of light. I cannot recall whether or not my dad and I made it outside before the strange light went away, but I am clear that an explosion and continuous rumbling like thunder miles away followed this temporary day.

Two thoughts rushed into my head as a boy of about eleven: Was this a nuclear war, or could it be the Second Coming of Christ? I was not sure which I dreaded more. Though this experience dates me in a way, in another, it registers Christian confusion about the expectation of Christ's coming.

Couched in a Gospel whose theme is God with Us, I suggest that the coming of the Lord is not to scare children. Rather, two things coexist in what we believe about the Second Coming. Put as questions, to whom does the future belong? And two, how do our expectation and preparation move us toward the unknown?

Jesus' cautionary statement, "Take heed that no one deceives you" (Matt 24:4), is most relevant. Couple that with, "concerning that day and hour, no one knows . . . only the Father" (Matt 24:36). Already false christs (Matt 24:5) and false prophets (Matt 24:11) were on the scene to take advantage of the shaken nation. Where meaning is threatened by chaos, powermongers will rise with false narratives of the divine purpose. We may imagine that this is purely a modern phenomenon, but it is as old as the landscape of Scripture.

Living with a sense of the Son of Man coming is a way of preparation and longing for the Savior, not foreknowledge of some secret time which only a few may know. One has to do with a way of life lived in faith that the future belongs to God. The other is nothing but proud pretense to know God's ways. The former lives from hope in God. The latter wrests the future from God's hands and twists humble expectation into false knowledge that can frighten and control.

I am aware that what I have written can sound abstract and unrelated to us. That is why I ask this question to bring it more into focus. What does it mean to live without a future that ushers in with God? In short, it is to separate meaning and purpose from any relationship to God, that is, from any transcendent reality.

A future without God affects human longing ("How long, O Lord"), depriving us of any desire for justice over wrong. A future without God affects human longing, depriving us of a love that lasts beyond our feeble efforts. We lose expectation of anything but our exaggerated powers to make the world what we want. When the chaos of corruption, rampant evil, and mass slaughter hold sway, the human heart loses traction to get beyond them.

Without such hope, our affections, moods, and feelings are truncated. There is nothing beyond one's self and the immediate world. There is nothing that is good and grand and global. There is nothing to gather human beings into a larger and harmonious community and creation into a purposeful destiny.

But by joining faith in Christ's coming with anticipation of Christmas, we are imbued by the Holy Spirit with an enduring hope. The season is more than a quantity of decorations and giftwrapping. Rather, they can be, not exhaustible and exhausting commodities, but signs of a world into which God comes.

Even in Caesar's world, there is yet a wondrous love. From the rubble of civilizations passing, there is yet a joy beyond measure. Through the continuous clash of egos and swords, there is a peace that passes our understanding. These do not represent a fantasy tableau of some wish world. They are the firstfruits of a new creation. In tough times, faith has fed on such fare. From the hope-filled horizon of God's coming, we may tremble in awe, but we do not cower in fear.

The story goes that there was once a plain over which the angels' sang and announced new birth. Magi came from the east and offered their gifts, and the greatest gift commissioned them to go into all the world. Despite every effort to undo the story, God continues with us on this journey. By and by, the kingdoms of this world will become the kingdom of our Lord and of the Christ who will reign with a holy love and an everlasting peace.

The Christ confession, said Jesus, did not come from within Peter alone, but was revealed to him by God. And upon Peter the rock, the story of God with Us has become the fabric and foundation of the church (Matt 16). Whatever chaos and meaninglessness threaten to destroy, the gates of hell will not overpower it.

As with the tragedy of 9/11, we need not shout the coming of Christ. We may say it quietly, almost under our breath like an elderly man I overheard at an Advent service: "I long for your glorious coming." And sometimes, we may need to whisper its truth as on the occasion of announcing a terminal disease or even a tentative first love. For those who have been scarred or traumatized, we may need simply to blanket such suffering with warmth, for what else can we do but take a small part in the story? We are not in control. Nonetheless, this quiet and persistent journey into the coming of God is what yet draws our lives from frightful and lonely places to Bethlehem.

CHAPTER SIXTEEN

To Imagine a Language

THERE IS A SAYING that faith is more caught than taught. I agree if by "caught" we mean that faith gets into us and becomes part of us as we practice it. While in seminary, I had the privilege of studying for a semester with a philosophical theologian by the name of Paul Holmer. He introduced us to the philosophy of Ludwig Wittgenstein.

On the final for that course, Holmer asked us to write a question that summarized what we had learned and to answer it. Mine was, "Wittgenstein wrote, 'To imagine a language means to imagine a form of life.'[1] What did he mean by that?"

I won't attempt to answer that question as if for a test. But it obviously has stuck with me. Wittgenstein used the image of "language games" to make his philosophy of language accessible. My illustration, not his: if I began to speak of foul balls, running the bases, an off-speed pitch, sliding into second, a pop-up, or a home run, what language would I be speaking? Of course, that of baseball.

One could read about these terms in a rule book of baseball, but most would agree that seeing a game at the park or on a screen would be a better way to understand the language. Others might say that you really cannot understand the game until you have played it at some level.

In this way a language, according to Wittgenstein, is inseparable from some form of life. Biblical scholars have rightly been critical of some attempts to move from dictionary definitions of words to how they are used in Scripture. The variety of uses in context is what informs the dictionary definitions. If one is interested, a delightful book by Simon Winchester, *The*

---

1. Wittgenstein, *Philosophical Investigations*, 8e.

Professor and the Madman, tells, in part, the story of how the Oxford Dictionary of the English Language came to be.

In traveling with Matthew, I have attempted to consider what his presentation of a narrated life of Jesus might mean for the congregations to which he wrote. Furthermore, since this Gospel writer was moving from a person in whom he had faith to comfort, challenge, and encourage those of a later generation, do we not have before us an example of someone moving out and into the future with the gospel message? Since the trajectory of the move is similar, whether to the late first century or the early twenty-first, what might we learn by following it closely?

Clearly in Matthew's Gospel as well as the whole of the New Testament, traveling with Jesus is not merely about a matter of interpreting texts. It is about following that person who moves within them. It is about learning to submit to the story as a story that can and will shape us. And the way that we go about doing this is in and through a community of persons who desire a form of life that brings the story to life in the contemporary world. Therefore, following Christ is about abiding in the story as it shows us who we are through loving God and loving our neighbors.

One congregation I served worshipped in a colonial-style meeting house built in 1825. The community had developed around it, so the corner on which our space existed became the busiest in that town. While I was there, we began to speak of "the church on the corner of the love of God and the love of neighbor." It was the way we spoke about ourselves, but it was also the way we aspired to live. Within that way of speaking and living, faith grew and shaped us.

How Matthew Shapes Faith

What kind of story is Matthew? The child Jesus has been born, and persons known as "magoi" (magi) journeyed to Jerusalem. We venture that they were astrologers of some kind, stargazers, looking for an appearance of anything noteworthy. Matthew doesn't give much background information.

Rather, he tells us they came from the east. More than likely they were Gentiles. Whatever else the special star they saw meant to them, they figured it to be a sign of one born King of the Jews. While they were poking around in Jerusalem with their questions, Herod got wind of them. Did his interest pique more that they were seeking a king (a political opponent), or that they had come to worship him (a focus of religious devotion)?

Matthew tells us about Herod without telling us about him. "He was troubled" by their search. "And all Jerusalem with him." When Herod ain't happy, nobody is happy. The Gentile magi were of one mind about this birth, but the Jewish king Herod, barely Jewish at that, was of another. It seems that Matthew had his number from what we know of Herod from other sources. But we don't have to leave the page to do a Wikipedia search. Matthew will show us what Herod was like.

To the point, lips dripping with deceit, Herod commands the foreign visitors to go seek diligently for the child and come back with news that he, too, might go and worship him. As the old preachers asked, "If the wise men were so smart, why did they tip off the likes of Herod?" But it's not hard to imagine two different kinds of smart: one bent on retaining power at all costs; the other in deep search of a reason to bend the knee.

They went on their way to Bethlehem. The star which seems to have waited for them to finish with Herod "led them on until it stood over the place where the child was" (Matt 2:9). "And seeing the star, they were overjoyed with an exceedingly great joy" (Matt 2:10). And we must pause.

In verse 9, Matthew tells us, "They set out; and there, ahead of them, went the star they had seen at its rising, until it stopped over the place where the child was." Why must the narrator repeat the obvious in the next verse, "and seeing the star"? My hunch is that he doesn't want us to miss the very heart of their journey and so the journey on which he wants to take us. And what is that?

The sum of it is packed into a sentence. As when the whole atmosphere is gathered up in a tornado wind, only this is a tornado of ecstasy that is about to envelope them, "seeing the star, they were overjoyed with an exceedingly great joy." If we cannot allow such a joy to stop us in our tracks and to tingle our spines and melt our hearts, we have not made it to Bethlehem. I believe that is what Matthew wants his readers to know. This is a story about an incredible joy.

Whether young or old or in between, when we contemplate the story of God with Us, we need to know that it is accompanied by an incredible joy. Matthew cannot pack more into his sentence than that "they were overjoyed with an exceedingly great joy."

He will tell us that this is about light in our darkness. It is about hope for our despair. It is about healing for our various diseases. It is about a shepherd for all our lost ways. It is about a kingdom for the poor, comfort for those who mourn, righteousness and justice for those who seek it. It is about compassion and grace and, above all, good news.

The star came from a far horizon and stood where the Christ child was. And it would return through the lips of the disciples to all nations to the close of the age. Do we not live between those horizons? This story encompasses our days.

And Yet

And yet, all is not peaches and cream. We must read on. The magi are warned in a dream not to return to Herod. And then Joseph is warned to take the child and mother to Egypt because Herod is about to destroy his competitor.

Then Herod, from his temper tantrum over being tricked by the magi, sends his goons to Bethlehem to kill all the boy babies from age two and down. This was to fulfill what Jeremiah the prophet spoke about Rachel. "A voice in Ramah was heard, weeping and great wailing, Rachel crying for her children, and she would not be comforted, for they were no more" (Jer 31:15).

Soon we are told that Herod died, and the angel appeared to Joseph with the message that he could return from Egypt to the land of promise with the child and Mary. Rather than go back to Judea where Archelaus, Herod's son, reigned in his place, they went north and settled in Nazareth in Galilee.

But we must not hurry to Galilee to bypass the Massacre of the Innocents which makes us so uncomfortable at Christmas. In the lectionary, following Christmas Day, it sits like a room full of opened gifts in an undulating sea of wrapping paper. Loose Scotch tape sticks to grandpa's slipper. And a bit off-balance he comes too close to the tree, causing dry evergreen needles to fall like a summer shower. Out in the fridge, much rewrapped and crinkled foil surrounds leftover turkey with a leg bone spotted as if trying to escape. And a small child's voice lingers in a parent's ears after the great rush at the tree and all the presents lie opened. "Is that all?"

What came with the ebb of such great expectations now flows with a squall of doldrums. It is the downside of Christmas.

Like so many worship planners, preachers, and church musicians, I have tried to manage the moods of Christmas. There are frequent warnings that for some the holidays are not happy. Not everyone is snuggled in a horse-drawn sleigh, riding up to the porch of a wreathed and festively-lit home. Welcoming faces peer through the glass out to the gently falling snow. Under a star, a handsome tree, laden with ornaments and shining with an aura of light, sits poised in the bay window. Such is what we see on television, but we are reminded that the forlorn, the homeless, the poor can neither relate to it nor partake of it.

Some have begun to plan services they call "Blue Christmas." They intend to be more sensitive to those for whom Advent/Christmas is a painful reminder of something. I have certainly heard elderly folk say, "This season is for children." But Matthew chapter 2 is not only for children. As we scroll down the page, there can be no G rating on account of the story's violence.

This chapter of a great journey and a holy birth holds both incredible joy together with abject sorrow. It is not unlike the whole of Matthew's Gospel.

It reminds me of those segments of the liturgy in the smaller congregations I have served when we ask for joys and concerns. One day we gave thanks for the birth of a child and marked the passing of an elderly saint. When tragedy rocked the community and yet we welcomed new members, someone would remark, "What a shame that one had to overshadow the other."

But where else than in church, in God's presence, can we bring both joy and sorrow? Years ago, the actor Peter Ustinov, who had won an Oscar for his performance in the movie *Spartacus*, answered critics about that film. Some thought that the humor of his character was out of place in a story about the freedom and tragedy of a slave rebellion. But Ustinov, in an interview which Google can access, reminded us that laughter and tears exist side by side in life.[2] Close to his exact words, it is silly to think that drama should be all funny or all serious. Comedy and tragedy are not that far removed from one another. As a friend, Victor L. Hunter says, "They are the two abiding theatrical masks of the drama of life."

The problem with Christmas in church may be the same, that we assume the liturgical seasons are all one thing or the other. I have had a similar reaction to persons who thought we should not exchange gifts and enjoy fine fare. In other words, I think it is wrong-headed to take away our feasts because there are those who famish. Instead, as do many congregations and parishes, we go about our celebrations by giving to others in need. Celebrating the gifts we have received, we open our hearts. Openness to God is a similar move to openness to others.

Where else but church do we celebrate the gifts of the magi on bended knee and gather offerings to give to the least of these? The story empowers us to deep joy and thanksgiving at the birth of Christ and to offer what we have and can for Christ in the faces of the hungry, thirsty, naked, the stranger, and those in prison. To dismiss this as "charity" as if we in churches cannot also back larger programs within the public and private sectors of our society is to miss the point. A story of deep gratitude and profound stewardship is what informs all we are and what we do. My concern is what happens to us as churches or our larger society when we no longer pay attention to a story like that.

---

2. Free Expression, "Peter Ustinov talks."

Over the years in confirmation classes, I brought from home a book by the children's author Mitsumasa Anno. Perhaps I have inappropriately designated him a children's author because what I am about to say is not only for children.

In *Anno's Italy*, a book mostly wordless, Anno gives us a travelogue of Italian culture in pictures.[3] On the first page, a figure whom we will trace throughout the book rows to the shore. In *Where's-Waldo* style, children on our laps delight to find Anno on each page. But for older children, there are scenes of Italy, its flora and fauna, its landscape, its architecture, its historical figures, its movie stars. To this day, I am sure I have missed some of the references.

Also, on almost each page, there is a scene from the Bible. Adam and Eve fleeing the garden in one corner. Magi on camels on another page. A mother with child near a small barn. Baptism of a long-haired, robed figure in a stream. These vignettes continue in chronological fashion as the pictures of Italy move from the bucolic countryside to a busy town center replete with flea market here and there a festive parade. Then out of town, we journey to the shore once again. Three empty crosses stand on the hillside, and nearby, the ancient pillars from the old Roman forum. There's a boat, reminiscent of the disciples going back to fishing, and Anno gets in his and away.

In sermons and confirmation classes, I have attempted the analogy. The story of God with Israel and God with Us in Jesus Christ abides on every page of our lives. It is not prominent in every place, but it is there. On some few pages, particularly the most busy ones, the Bible story is not visible to my eye. But turning the page, we pick up its thread. Just as the story of Italian culture cannot be told without the biblical story of God, so our lives are interwoven with it. Sometimes it is lost to us, but turning a page, we may pick it up again.

"To imagine a language means to imagine a form of life." I can give reasons for why I believe, and I have. But the way faith has gotten inside me and won't go away is like the story of Matthew that holds incredible joy with abject sorrow in the welcoming and hope-filled, suffering and life-giving heart of God with Us.

Hope and Grapple

Yet, on the busy pages, Anno is lost to us. In a similar way, the story can recede from view among the welter of things to do and the demands we feel.

3. Anno, *Anno's Italy*.

In the modern church, we are expected to be about justice for all, programs for all, awareness of all.

My wife and I attended a committee of our presbytery not long after we had become Presbyterians. Its title may have been "Church and Society." The agenda was to walk through a list of concerns, everything from better practices to care for the earth to justice issues around gay and lesbian persons. Also on the docket were particular local ways to address hunger, homelessness, housing, racism, equality for women, reproductive rights, alternatives to abortion, and the like

We went home with vertigo. This was only one range of topics facing the church. In those days, I served a small congregation. We did not have committees or enough people to accept responsibility to look into seventeen different areas of church and society, not to mention education, evangelism, mission/outreach, spirituality, stewardship, and worship, each with its own range of topics. Vertigo settled into its chair, sinking into a mild depression.

I felt like the man in his old truck who was passed on the highway by a shiny, speeding BMW. When down the road he was towed into a service station totally bedraggled, bruised, and bleeding, the woman who had been driving the Beemer was just coming out of the restaurant next door. "What happened to you?" she asked the man. "Well, back there when you passed me so fast, I thought I was stopped and got out to see what was the matter."

How does one respond to Christ's call in an environment that demands we be about all things at once? How does one deal with the feeling of not knowing nearly enough when there are so many disparate things to know that it would take an encyclopedic mind to hold them all together?

The other piece of this predicament is more than juggling knowledge, competence, and time. It is that we feel compromised by a society in which we, too, are caught up in the problems we seek to address. In small churches, for example, pastors have felt guilty when the choice is between increasing the mission budget or providing a raise for the pastor. It is the pastor who has been preaching about the church following Christ into the world, and yet her family has not had money to go on vacation for the past three years.

We take to heart the challenging words of Jesus in Matthew "to sell all you have and give it to the poor and come follow me" (Matt 19:21). We have in our minds those words, "if any want to follow me, let them deny self, take up the cross and follow me" (Matt 16:24). "Love your enemies," (Matt 5:9) eschew divorce (Matt 5:31,32), turn the other cheek (Matt 5:39). "Enter through the narrow gate" (Matt 7:13).

And here we sit with a multi-millionaire, afraid to ask for $50,000 for the capital campaign. Or, we find ourselves advising the steeple repair committee on work which will cost three times as much as the total mission/

outreach budget for the next five years. Or, the federal government has recently decided to remove seven hundred thousand people from social services and instead wants to decrease taxes for the very richest citizens. All the while, biblical texts sting the conscience when our thoughts turn to the wealthy Joneses who quite possibly will quit the congregation if we but lift a "non-partisan" moral voice in the name of Christ.

It can seem to us that the way we have to go is itself cluttered with obstacles, caked with grime. Must we inevitably be tainted by the world, even we who live out our vocation within the precincts of the church? The hermeneutic of suspicion would cast us all as somehow caught in this tangled web. How do we serve a higher calling in the trenches of ministry?

In a marvelous piece of reflection on the concept of calling, the theologian Emil Brunner observed that God "relieves [the one called] from the responsibility for this place in the world which, as such—like all places, like every form of time and place in the historical world—is not holy, but sinful . . . every definite place, every definite set of circumstances in which we have to act, if it be considered on its merits, would not bear too close an ethical examination. In order to act with a good conscience I would always be obliged first of all to seek another place; or I could never act with a good conscience. But the Divine Call demands actions here and now, and for this reason it gives the good conscience as well; and this good conscience, in spite of the bad place in or at which one has to act, is only possible through the idea of the Calling."[4]

As to where we must walk in following Christ in the world, Brunner says, "the place is 'pure'—however bad it may be in itself. It is 'pure' through the Call of God. And this paradoxical purity, this making holy of that which in itself is unholy, through God's forgiving call: this is the Calling."[5]

Moses before the burning bush was made to remove the sandals from his feet because the ground on which he stood was holy. It was holy, not because it was pure, but because God was there.

The ground we tread in following Christ is not pure or impure of itself, but pure because Christ walks there. God with Us goes before us in the way. And though we like those first disciples follow from a great distance, by his calling and forgiving love, we walk in confidence that the Calling of God has made the way for us. That he is the Way does not mean "my way or the highway." It means that folk the likes of us cannot travel of our own accord without it being a hallowed way. Otherwise, we become paralyzed in heart, mind, and will.

---

4. Brunner, *Divine Imperative*, 201.

5. Brunner, *Divine Imperative*, 201.

Our grappling in hope concerns the way of ministry that is cluttered and compromised. Especially therein, we need trust that God is with us. God hallows the way, that is, frees us to walk where we are. No one can get on her horse and set off in all directions at once. No one can step out on an absolutely pure path. We need God's grace to begin and to take steps without the burden of clearing the way before we can walk it.

CHAPTER SEVENTEEN

Gathering Threads within a Theme

NOT TO REPEAT EVERYTHING, but to reemphasize, Matthew is an elegant and coherent presentation of the life of Jesus of Nazareth. No wonder that it was placed first among the four Gospels and brought so many in the ancient world to Christ.[1]

When I say that Matthew is a life of Jesus, I mean in the sense of that unique literary type that became known as a "Gospel." It was and is unique because Jesus looms large as its subject and its message. The anonymous author does not presume to get Jesus right by piling detail upon detail about Jesus' life. In fact, bits that might interest us may yet remain on the cutting room floor. Rather, what the evangelist wanted readers to know was governed by memory of a sacred past and what had gripped them about it, not a voyeuristic visit backstage.

Once again, anonymous authorship should not be understood out of its biblical context. Where we want to make sure that everything anyone has written is properly attributed, they may have thought of themselves as writing in the tradition of Isaiah, Matthew, Paul, and others. Arguably the most soaring passages of Scripture in Isaiah 40–55 were not written by Isaiah of Jerusalem in the 8th century BCE but placed without seam or notoriety in the tradition of Isaiah.

Within this study, I have made comments like the above to address questions I and others have asked about the nature of biblical literature, not to advance a new scholarly notion about them. My point of view in these pages has been to clear our minds of any intimidation we might feel

---

1. Brown, *Introduction*, 171, 208.

from the scholars so that we may truly benefit from their work (though not always agreeing) and neither denigrate them nor ignore them. Enough said.

To the Heart

At the heart of Matthew is the theme of God with Us. It is stated explicitly in the beginning, middle, and end of the gospel. But it does not leave us even though the phrase is not reiterated in every passage. The theme's nature as bookends or an implicit frame for the Gospel guided Matthew's first readers and guides us still if we will let it.

Guiding us through the seasons of life may be an overworked metaphor, but I use it here because Matthew clearly takes us on a kind of journey with Jesus, who calls us to follow. Rounding out our traveling with Matthew, let's first consider the literal seasons of the Christian Year, Advent to Advent. It takes its themes from the order of the four Gospels. In addition there are biblical and theological themes such as Good Shepherd, Trinity, and Christ the King Sundays, plus free time to do what we choose with the days and given texts known as Ordinary Time.

I came to these seasons from a very iconoclastic tradition in which we eschewed all holy days but the Lord's Day because they were not mentioned per se in Scripture. This is one example of how, trying to be strictly biblical, we nearly suffocated the religious motivation to embrace the faith in actual time and space.

It was a cold December night upstate New York when I, as a young minister, was traveling by car under a vast ceiling of stars and listening to Christmas carols on the radio. In that moment I flipped from being averse to the religious celebration of Christmas to become a full-fledged practitioner of the Christian year.

I wanted to sing those great carols full-throated with all their Christian significance. I wanted to smell the evergreen in church, to light Advent candles, to see and wear all the liturgical colors, to celebrate and partake of communion on Christmas Eve, at Easter, and on Pentecost. Though I did not begin to do all of these at once, my lonely heart that night in New York was suddenly opened to the worldwideness of the church's journey through the Christian year, the lectionary being its roadmap. God with Us on every page and in every season brought the story home to me in music, color, taste, chart, and compass.

Traveling with Matthew, we are opened, less literally, to a season of wonder and discovery. The journey of the magi (Matt 2) takes us from some far-distant horizon to a starlit destination. It has variously been described by the great poets: "A cold coming we had of it, just the worst time of year for a journey, and such a long journey" (T. S. Eliot, in part quoting Lancelot Andrewes).[2] "Led by the light of an unusual star, we hunted high and low, Have traveled far" (Auden),[3] while Yeats concludes the magi's search with "The uncontrollable mystery on the bestial floor."[4] As the poets see it, these were persons going the long way beyond all other pursuits, and finding its end both disturbing and knee-bending. Matthew fuels our imagination.

No less so than Jesus' words in the Sermon on the Mount, "Ask, seek, knock" (Matt 7), direct us to God's bounty and exhort us to persistence. There is a greater dimension to our existence than youthful boredom and age-ladened sadness that Jesus invites us to explore continually. The journey is not some one-and-out Herculean effort but an ongoing lifting of the heart.

In the middle, Matthew offers us a marvelous chapter on practical matters such as forgiving the repeat sinner and being reconciled with someone who sins against the church. Jesus transfers authority to even two or three gathered in his name. "There I am in their midst" (Matt 18: 20).

Though not always interpreting the passage in the context of church disagreements, many Christians have wondered about the divine presence of Christ in their midst. I believe that Matthew and Jesus give us full license. God with Us is the Sacred Between of our existence.

But it is not as I have heard about religious twosomes who placed a Bible on the front seat of a car between them to remind them of the distance they should keep. Admittedly we can get carried away in forbidding all intimacy in relationships. Nonetheless, the Sacred Between is a powerful symbol of who we are in relationships, even in keeping boundaries. Personhood is never to be reduced to raw power over one another.

At the same time, It is not to be taken for granted, as in refusing to see life from one another's perspective even after years of being together. We are continually "to welcome one another just as Christ has welcomed us" (Rom 15:7) The Sacred Between of Matthew is not some kind of rule enforcer but an entre into the mystery of persons among whom God has deigned to be present. God with Us is a kind of sacred dimension, God enfleshed and hallowing earthly, even earthy, existence and calling us onto holy ground. And so, we wonder, explore and discover.

---

2. Eliot, *Poems and Plays*, 68–69.
3. Auden, *Longer Poems*, 171–172.
4. Yeats, *Selected Poems*, 49.

Another Season

"Seeing the crowd round about, Jesus was filled with compassion because they were harassed and helpless like sheep without a shepherd" (Matt 9:36). This verse may be more descriptive of Jesus' ministry taken as a whole as opposed to a straightforward travel narrative. "Jesus went about all the cities and towns, teaching in their synagogues, proclaiming the good news of the kingdom and healing every disease and infirmity" (Matt 9:35). In other words, he was among the people, teaching, preaching, healing. Which leads Matthew to comment that Jesus was deeply moved. The Greek word "splachnizomai" captures the sense of what is felt deep in one's gut where emotions reside. Again the word occurs in Matthew 14:14 when Jesus "saw a great crowd and had compassion for them. He healed their diseases." Soon thereafter, he fed them.

There is a wholeness of human need that moves Jesus. Given some of our backgrounds, it is not an abstract lost soul in danger of eternal torment. Rather, Jesus walks among us and feels what we feel. He teaches, proclaims good news and heals all manner of human woundedness.

Then he says to his disciples, "Great is the harvest, but the workers are few. Pray, therefore, that the Lord of the harvest will send out workers into the Lord's harvest" (Matt 9:37). And here I would like to redeem an old word.

The NRSV felicitously translates that "Jesus was filled with compassion" because the people "were harassed and helpless" (Matt 9:36.) One could just as easily translate the participles as "vexed or troubled" and "scattered." But I like the alliteration which speaks to me of a kind of lostness today that is different than "a lost soul headed for hell."

There are so many lost persons buffeted by life and without a compass to guide them. One church I served housed a Parent's Support Group for those with children suffering addiction. Though addiction recovery pursues many paths, the Alcoholics Anonymous movement has stressed the importance of a strong spiritual component to recovery. Years ago "hopeless drunk" was a common phrase. The Twelves Steps have been for countless millions a way to find hope again.

In a similar vein, a wonderful therapist once said, "I can give people strategies for how to live. I cannot give them a reason to live." Other perspectives are necessary that open to greater dimensions.

Such dimension and depth can be lost to view. I once talked heart to heart with a pastor in Cuba. His assessment was that between Marxist materialism and capitalist materialism there wasn't much difference between Cuban and US societies. We were not discussing the relative merits of political freedom, simply the value placed on things alone to deliver human well-being.

Well-being is one way of translating the biblical "shalom," which addresses fullness or completeness of life. In a shalom-like way, Jesus' ministry relates the good news of the kingdom directly to healing. The Greek words for "healing" and "saving" in the New Testament are not so far apart in their usage as are the way we use the English words. In fact, human beings in Scripture are thought to be more of a psychosomatic unity than our tendency to separate body and mind. Jesus' summary of the law, quoting Deuteronomy, gathers up heart, self/soul, mind (Matt 22:37) into the love of God. Mark and Luke include "strength" in the mix. In other words, one's whole person.

Perhaps the lost today are those of us who have no shepherd to guide us toward that great reality that knits us together as we were created to be. There is no legitimate separation between treating our sickness and feeding our thirst for justice. There is no legitimate separation between lifting our hearts to something truly good and feeding, clothing, and housing our bodies.

In the lost seasons of our lives, we are fragmented, torn apart among so many things, so many demands and options. And at the same time, we are reduced to a kind of flatline living by the criteria of quantification. "Harassed and helpless" gets at it. Or, "come unto me all you who are weary and heavy laden" (Matt 11).

Seasons Are Like Angles of Vision

Matthew shines the light of God with Us, radiating hope for those who sit in darkness. (Matt 4) The first gospel makes directional sense in that light moves toward and illuminates the dark, not the reverse. We hear the same directional emphasis in the Beatitudes, blessings or gracious favor for the poor in Spirit (Matt 5). Jesus' insistence on obeying the Law with his lead phrase, "You have heard it say, but I say to you" may seem to us at first blush, a kind of unreachable plateau (Matt 5:27). Certainly a daunting moral stature may be understood in the words, "You shall be perfect as your heavenly father is perfect" (Matt 5:48). But that is to reverse the direction of grace, even to ignore the Beatitudes themselves.

Rather, the direction of light and grace is to open possibilities for those like the Gentiles upon whose situation of darkness Isaiah and Matthew announced the dawning of a new day. Similarly, grace for the poor in Spirit announced that ordinary people, not only those who rigorously attended to racial, religious, and ritual purity, could stand on their own two feet before God.

In other words, God favored them as well. There was no distinction in status between some first-class Jews and all the rest. Though God's perfection was high above them, God's favor dignified their reach. By placing their and our existence radically before God, Jesus does not set up a competition or scheme of comparison among those who follow him. He did not like it when the disciples fell into this kind of argument. "Whoever desires to be first among you must be your servant" (Matt 20:27). As Bornkamm puts it so well, the marks of righteousness are not "what we put on display as in a shop window."[5] "Pray in secret. Do not disfigure your faces as if fasting" (Matt 6:6, 16).

Each day we rise again to our full height as human beings, the persons God created us to be. Thereby we learn God's strength and purpose and the courage to be our best selves. And what better way than in that magisterial "language game" of the kingdom, learning to love God with our whole being and likewise, our neighbors as ourselves (Matt 22)?

Misreadings of Matthew come up with a legalistic Gospel. But that is to reverse the order of God's light and grace and compassion, imagining God as the "out-to-getcha" deity that the hiding, one-talent servant did. His was a total misperception of God as one who looks for growth where no seeds have been planted (Matt 25). Not a few blame imagined or real persons and forces for their intransigence. Not a few cower before responsibility due to hellish circumstances, imagined or real. Though the journey back from hell is not easy to take, it should not be compounded by refusing the direction of mercy, which is to seek and save the lost, not to pin us on a board as if we were insects in an experimental laboratory.

To view Christ with Matthew's angle of vision is to keep in mind the self-giving nature of God, the bounty of God. Many a fresh start has begun, realizing that Christ is not a taskmaster or taskmistress standing over us with a whip in hand but "the Son of Man [who] who came not to be served but to serve, and to give his life as a ransom for many" (Matt 20:28).

Chaos on the Brink of Despair

Matthew journeys into chaos, despair, and meaningless in the company of the coming Son of Man. With a brief summary of the Jewish War with the Romans, I attempted to indicate the terror taken from that time into Matthew's poetic depictions of the end. It was not the end of the space/time

---

5. Bornkamm, *Jesus of Nazareth*, 85.

universe, but the tragic end of an era. Some of those who heard or read this Gospel may have actually fled for their lives and known others who did not escape.

Drawing on Bernhard Anderson's powerful discussion of Isaiah 40–55, I suggested a similar theological shift in Matthew. One can use the conceptual scheme of God's punishment for sin until the burden of suffering tilts the balance of justification too far to make sense of it. Hence the shift to the suffering servant of Isaiah who on God's behalf bore the weight of sin (Isa 53). In a similar way, Jesus saves by taking on himself the unbearable burden. His blood is shed on the cross as the temple curtain is torn in two. No sacrifice made there could set to rights the evil afflicted on its steps or on humankind. Only suffering taken on by God with Us could symbolize the broken heart at the heart of all.

There is no scheme of problem/solution that addresses what earth suffers. But to hear a despairing cry from the cross, "My God, my God, why have you forsaken me?" (Matt 27:46) places God squarely where sense-making cannot go. It is the mystery of God's presence in the season of suffering and despair that raises this story from the abyss to unimaginable heights.

Hope and Grapple

As we gather the threads of Matthew within the theme of God with Us, we may better understand how the Pharisees represent a contrast or foil to Jesus' mission and ministry. We might continue our metaphor of seasons by calling this "the season of refocus."

In chapter 13 I accented the difference Jesus had with the Pharisees by referring to two great stories. I recall here only the story that can be traced to Ezra/Nehemiah. The other I called "Matthew and the Story of Light."

In brief, Ezra and Nehemiah represent a kind of circling of the wagons in a reset of Jewish faith and practice. They believed that God had punished Israel for disobedience to the covenant by raising up the Babylonians who sacked Jerusalem and took numerous captives to a foreign land. This was known as "the deportation" or "the exile."

The prophets had, in fact, excoriated the people for forsaking YHWH, the Lord. With the edict of Cyrus (538 BCE) and the return of the exiles, Ezra and Nehemiah doubled down on racial purity, regulating ritual, and a religious understanding of Jewish identity as uniquely, even exclusively, related to the biblical God.

During the independence of the Maccabees from Syrian domination, a similar separatist movement arose. Quite possibly it came to be called

"Pharisee" due to this separatism, but regardless of the etymology of the word, the Pharisees represent another reset, emphasizing racial, religious, and ritual observance.

As Gerd Theissen so rightly observes, this strain of Jewish belief and practice was born out of a concern for greater faithfulness to YHWH by way of a passionate desire to be the people YHWH wants.[6] Threats to assimilate and to become a people mixed with the nations cut Jewish identity to the quick. It is hard to overstate in this form of Judaism the overlap of Jewish faith and identity. In shorthand, these are the signs of its observance: ritual cleansing, eating with other pure Jews, keeping a kosher kitchen and table, keeping one's distance from defilement in public life. I emphasize that these are not some program of works righteousness. They are marks and reminders of the people's devotion to God and determination never again to forsake the God of Israel.

Christians have sometimes been critical of the Pharisees in the New Testament, as if they were religious lightweights or even silly. This is neither true nor fair. The Pharisees and their predecessors had suffered a great deal and so had rededicated themselves to God with a thoroughgoing seriousness of devotion.

Over against this, Matthew portrays the Pharisees as taking themselves too seriously in wearing their religion on their sleeves, so to speak. This is a rather human foible of which all religious people have been guilty. But in Matthew 23, Jesus shows respect for the office of the scribes and Pharisees as teachers in Israel. "Whatever they say, do and keep" (Matt 23:3). But Jesus continues, "According to their works, do not do, because they say and do not or, they say one thing and do another" (Matt 23:3).

At this point, we may hear in the biblical text a rather modern understanding of hypocrisy. A hypocrite is someone who is not genuine because he or she pretends to be something by public profession which behavior behind the scenes belies.

In the ancient Greek world, a hypocrite was simply an actor who used a mask in a given role, but behind the mask was who he or she actually was. "Hypocrite" did not have a negative connotation. It referred to an actor who, under the mask, was playing a part in the theatre.

I suggest that the way Jesus in Matthew 23 and elsewhere uses the word "hypocrite" may indicate a person of a different kind of religion rather than one who is not religiously genuine. And this different kind of religion derives from one tradition of faith and practice which we have been considering above.

---

6. Theissen, *Early Palestinian Christianity*, 77.

To be as clear as I can, allow me to contrast two modern expressions. One, "He does not practice what he preaches." This gets at our popular view of a hypocrite as someone who is not genuine. But the Pharisees, as I understand them, were, indeed, practicing what they preached.

Another expression, "She is making a mountain out of a molehill." This has nothing to do with not being genuine. Rather, the saying points to an exaggeration of something(s) that are not of equal importance to others. The truth of this saying aligns more with Jesus' criticism of the Pharisees. "You tithe dill, mint, and cummin, but you neglect the weightier matters of the law, justice, faith, and mercy. Blind guides, those who strain out the gnat, but swallow the camel" (Matt 23:23–24).

Earlier in the chapter, Jesus admonishes them for "binding heavy burdens and placing them on people's shoulders." All the while, they do not lift a finger to remove those burdens (Matt 23:4). Can we imagine that in their efforts to achieve a pure identity before God, the Pharisees had equated lesser and greater religious practices? Perhaps they had lost the proper distinction between the superficial and the substantive.

I am indebted to the work of Davies and Allison: "If Jesus' commandments are 'light' (Matt 11:30; 1 John 5:3), those of his opponents are, by implication 'heavy.' The reader inevitably thinks of the halakhic rules Jesus counters in chapters 12 and 15. Even so, as Calvin . . . realized, it is not a question of hard rules versus easy rules or even more versus less. The Sermon on the Mount, especially 5:20, blasts that notion. The opponents' yoke is so heavy probably because: (i) as Matt 23:23 avows, it takes insufficiently into account justice, mercy, and faith; (ii) its proponents, as the next line states, lift no finger to help . . . and [perhaps] (iii) the application of the purity laws to everyday life is toilsome to the uninitiated (that is, non-Pharisees)."[7]

Translated into our modern context, if we do not keep to the deeper, more essential matters, we can take our eyes off God and focus way too much on ourselves. Desiring to be seen and to have the first seats (Matt 23:5–6), are these not ways that the Pharisees allowed their view of righteousness to make themselves the focus of righteousness? Isn't there a link to praying at an out-of-the-way place rather than on a street corner (Matt 6: 5–8)? Also, what of making up one's face to exaggerate the appearance of fasting rather than washing to look normal (Matt 6:16–18)?

Perhaps they wanted to show others the importance of praying, fasting, wearing their faith in public? But they had taken their eyes off the prize. The prophet Micah had said, "What does the Lord require of you but to do

---

7. Davies and Allison, *Matthew*, Vol. III, 272.

justice, to love kindness, and to walk humbly with God?" (Mic 6: 8). Is Jesus not getting at the same thing here?

In an effort to increase or restore the church's profile in society, we can be consumed by its relative membership size and its media prestige and lose sight of the truth that God's mission is for the life of the world, not making an empire of the church. In an effort to enact justice in effective, practical ways, we can fly the banners of our social agendas or imitate political leaders who can no longer confess their sins.

G. K. Chesterton once said, "As much as I ever did, more than I ever did, I believe in liberalism. But there was a rosy time of innocence when I believed in liberals."[8] Conservatives, liberals, corporate executives, prominent politicians, pastors, priests, rabbis, imams, elders, deacons, and such like, we all have sinned. We all have feet of clay. We all are earthenware vessels. The treasure that abides us is what makes us. The story of God with Us is what we are about. There is only one who is worthy of our bent knees and the humility of our hearts. Justice, faith, and mercy focus us, not on our being religious, but on the God who keeps us in our being and doing.

---

8. G.K. Chesterton, *Orthodoxy*, 46.

CHAPTER EIGHTEEN

Back to the Beginning and with God to the Future

A PROJECT LIKE THIS cannot be drawn to a close because Matthew itself is open-ended. We are invited to join the journey and go where it takes us. But to say that is to remember where we began. It was in the swamp of those begats which we learned have purpose.

From the first chapter and its first few verses, Matthew was reaching back to bring an old story forward. He was retelling the story of Israel and centering it around Jesus of Nazareth.

From his announced theme, "Emmanuel, which means, 'God is with us,'" he draws upon Isaiah in particular and the Hebrew Bible generally to tell his readers who Jesus was and is. I quoted the scholar Richard Hays who took us back to Genesis 28 in the Septuagint where Jacob pillows his head on a stone. There he dreams of a ladder or stairway set up on earth, reaching to heaven, with the angels of God ascending and descending it. God's voice speaks in the dream, "Know that I am with you and will keep you wherever you go" (Gen 28:15). Professor Hays notes that the Greek of the Septuagint in Genesis 28 is nearly identical to Matthew's Greek in Matthew 28, "I am with you to the close of the age" (Matt 28:20).

At this place, which became known as Bethel, meaning "house of God," Jacob realizes the presence of God for his hazardous journey. He was running from his past under the cloud of a murderous threat by his brother Esau. He was going to a land and people he did not know with the feeble assurances of his mother Rebekah that her people would treat him well.

Matthew recenters this old story around Jesus, the story of the people Israel, Jacob being their namesake. The evangelist addressed this Gospel to communities of faith in Jesus who lived in the first century, possibly the 80s or 90s CE. As mostly Jewish Christians, their world had fallen apart during the Jewish War with Rome. They faced a future unmoored from their past, uncertain what their future in a mostly Gentile world might hold. For this fledgling company of Jewish Jesus followers, given that Gentiles were now joining their ranks, would this uncertain path force them once again to assimilate or would they somehow be guided by the great Law of Moses? Matthew addresses all of their concerns.

As for us, we live in a time when the old story is less well known. Even for those of us who attend worship or mass with some regularity, there are many competing narratives which threaten to drown out the theme of God with Us that runs through the pages of our lives.

Like those movie audiences who first greeted the new camera techniques of Orson Welles and Gregg Toland with great enthusiasm, our eyes and minds are constantly at work surveying the world like a movie screen to make sense of it. They do so at the most basic level of bringing the house across the street into focus. And they also strive to make sense of the vastly complicated landscape of modern life.

Traveling with Matthew is a kind of lens for seeing our world in divine light. By it we are reminded that God is with us in incredible moments of joy and through the wailing of abject sorrow. What other story holds life together and embraces us in such a way?

I have come to believe that no argument for God's existence keeps me, but rather, there's a presence that stays with us. But as Yeats put it, that presence is "the uncontrollable mystery on the bestial floor."[1] We cannot command God, nor can we conjure God. We can only seek to be with God as God is with us. The old invitation is fresh as it once was, "Come to me, all you who are weary and heavy laden, and I will give you rest" (Matt 11:28).

ONE LAST HOPE AND GRAPPLE

Traveling with Matthew is a study, engaging with the Gospel for a purpose. That is, to better understand this portion of Scripture as God's Word for the church and society today.

The guiding assumption is that Matthew (the anonymous author) has narrated a story about Jesus of Nazareth who is Emmanuel, God with Us. "God with Us" is not only Matthew's explicit theme in 1:23; 18:20; 28:20, but is also implied throughout.

---

1. Yeats, *Selected Poems*, 49.

Inferred from the first Gospel, the audience is a community(ies) of mostly Jewish Christians with a smaller number of Gentiles having joined them. The exact percentage is not important, but the implied Jewish background of those to receive the message can be traced throughout Matthew.

A scholarly consensus dates Matthew and its readership to about the 80s into the 90s of the first century CE. This serves up the question, "What does Matthew want to bring forward from Jesus who lived, died, and was raised about fifty years prior for a community of faith who may still be struggling with the aftermath of the Jewish War with Rome (66CE to 73CE)?"

Given that Matthew affords a coherent message, drawing on a sacred past and relating it to Jesus followers some fifty years on, do we not have a trajectory of application to follow into our own day? To attempt a plausible response to that question, it is necessary that we stay with and follow closely this one Gospel.

That does not mean we cannot follow where Matthew leads us to passages and traditions in the Old Testament. Neither does it mean we cannot consider the other three Gospels and the rest of the New Testament in passages that relate to teachings and events referenced by Matthew. Relevant history and extrabiblical texts are also quite valuable as they pertain to the first Gospel's story.

Admittedly, our scope is on and through the lens of Matthew. But to engage with a portion of Scripture does not mean that we are generating a Matthean theology that has nothing to do with the rest of the New Testament. Though I believe Matthew offers a unique perspective, I do not believe that it strains the wider biblical or theological picture of Jesus of Nazareth.

Indicative of that, I have not pressed for a coherence of Matthew or Jesus Christ, for that matter, which is airtight. In my view, too literal and merely rational readings can be suffocating. As G.K. Chesterton contrasted the poet with the logician, I had rather us get our heads into the heavens than try to stuff heaven into our heads.[2] We must always leave room for the Spirit to move among us that we may breathe deeply as we read Scripture. Practically that means admitting that we may never fully understand a certain passage or that we must allow two texts that seem to contradict to sit side by side. The weakness of gospel harmonies was not allowing for different perspectives, leaving readers with the feeling that authors were trying to smash square pegs into round holes.

At the same time, it is my view that the differences posed between the Jesus of the Gospels and Christ Jesus of the apostle Paul have been exaggerated. Though Matthew and Paul, for example, are clearly coming at the

---

2. Chesterton, *Orthodoxy*, 17–18.

Law of Moses from different interpretive directions, their different angles of vision do not represent competing visions.

As a pastor and preacher, my penchant has been to understand persons and texts in their contexts. Once we do that, tensions may still exist, but holding them together serves rather than obscures understanding. Barry Johnson has offered a theory of conflict management that introduces interdependent polar opposites.[3] These follow the cycles of persons and organizations through fresh and stale periods, for example. The differences between them are not contradictions because they consist of who individuals are, even the same individuals, as life varies through time. Is it a renewing time or a conserving time? There are upsides and downsides to both, and we move from one to the other and back again.

This consists with the Word of God being dynamic, not static. It takes part in the dynamics of life and need not be fixed or limited to certain positions or situations. Efforts to nail God's Word down are like the crucifixion itself and must follow the story through to the resurrection which is the ultimate work beyond human control.

I accent a few interpretive principles that have guided me. First, let us allow Matthew to be Matthew. How Matthew relates the gospel is what we should follow in understanding the evangelist's message. This is why I began, as does Matthew, with the story of Israel that the author brings forward in the first few chapters, placing Jesus the Savior as its focus and centerpiece.

Second, the theme of the Savior from the beginning begs that we allow Matthew to articulate what the people need in a savior. With this and other thematic pieces, we should be careful not to impose views that are foreign to the text. Salvation is a large concept in Matthew that has the whole people in view. I believe that continues through to Jesus on the cross who sheds his blood as a sacrifice for the people even as the curtain in the temple is torn from top to bottom.

Third, Matthew, like Luke, begins the Beatitudes with Jesus saying, "blessed are the poor in Spirit" (Matt 5:3). Luke says, "blessed are the poor" (Luke 6:20). I think the difference between the two is not much if any, given the Gospels as a whole. Matthew throughout is concerned for us to see Jesus from the perspective of those in need. "I have come to call not the righteous but sinners" (Matt 9:13). We may say that Jesus in Matthew, like much of the rest of the New Testament, values humility as the vantage point to receive him, whether it be a humility of circumstances or a humility of mind and heart or both.

---

3. Johnson, *Polarity Management*.

Fourth, I have emphasized a directional reading of Matthew. It moves from light to darkness: "The people who sat in darkness have seen a great light" (Matt 4:16). And it moves from God's favor to human need. The Beatitudes are essentially words of blessing (God's favor, grace) upon those whom some of the most religious of that day viewed as not part of the authentic people of God or even outcasts from their viewpoint of the Law. In this same respect, Matthew, ironically as the most Jewish of the Gospels, is arguably the most clear in suiting Jesus in the role of Isaiah's servant. "I will give you as a light to the nations" (Isa 49: 6).

This directional emphasis is most necessary to understand as we follow Jesus' compassion, healing, good news, walking among the very needy, encountering women, children, and sinners. Truly there are lurid images of hell with which I have acknowledged my struggles. But reading backwards from gehenna and the weeping and gnashing of teeth to impose those images upon either Jesus or the Father does not sit well with Matthew.

In the parable of the talents, for example, the person who hid the gift from the master totally misunderstood the nature of the gift giver. Understanding God as bountiful, compassionate, gracious, forgiving, and not "out-to-getcha" has its home in Matthew.

Several of the parables, and Matthew in general, confront a narrow understanding of a god who will not open the kingdom to a great variety of people. Taken in this sense, I believe that the language of gehenna and weeping and gnashing in Matthew is not to fix us or God into a kind of hellish mentality toward others but to show the seriousness of separating ourselves or anyone else from the merciful nature of God.

Lastly, I do not offer my views of Matthew as the final word, probably not even my final word. What I have dedicated myself to do is a reading that does justice to the text itself. It is a reading informed by quality scholarship that contextualizes Matthew in its habitat of ancient cultures. It can be evaluated by others traveling with Matthew as the evangelist guides them.

Though no one can get inside Jesus' or Matthew's head, nor can we take a time machine to the first century, I am persuaded that approximate sense can be made of the first Gospel. Such principles of interpretation as these can lead us to a plausible understanding of Jesus of Nazareth.

The ultimate principle is the Galilean who is the divine porch on which we stand to "ask, seek, knock." A bountiful deity opens to the discovery of treasure, a pearl of the greatest value. Baptized in the crystal waters of the Triune God, we are made to drink of the story that centers and shapes our lives, God with Us to the close of the age.

EPILOGUE

On Going out the Door

LIKE ANY PREACHER ACROSS the years, I have heard some interesting takes on sermons while greeting people in the narthex on their way out. In most cases I could not correct what they thought they heard, nor could I make clearer what I thought I had said. But here, if you have gotten this far, I will briefly make the effort.

Two questions have been our traveling companions for Traveling with Matthew: 1) How does a gospel mean? and 2) In what ways and with what reach does Jesus in Matthew show that God is with us?

As we exit the narthex of this study, I move from the interpretive principles that have guided me in reading Matthew (chapter 18) to a more urgent statement about why Traveling with Matthew matters. Not that I haven't addressed these concerns already, but I gather here a sampler to reemphasize that the head is related to the heart, and what goes on in the church house is part and parcel of God's mission in the world outside. The two are inextricably related in God's story.

How does a Gospel mean puts the focus on *the literary Matthew*, the whole Gospel we have in our hands, not some breakdown or reconstruction of it. We have good reason to believe that in Matthew, we are being led by a competent and skillful guide to encounter Jesus Christ.

Beginning with a caravan of persons from Israel's past, Matthew brings the old story of God with Israel forward with a purpose. Not leaving that story behind as he introduces the gospel of Christ is most important for the evangelist. Jesus' identity works its way through and cannot be separated from the narrative that Matthew unfolds. In short, the identity of Jesus Christ is a narrated identity, a story that began with Israel, a story that opens with greater dimensions, a story about God's people on a journey.

Story shapes identity. Without a great story to live by, we easily lose who we are and whatever purpose in living we might have. Among the many fragments that modern life can hack us into, we can be made truly human by the power of a story to restore us to wholeness. The Gospel speaks most profoundly to why we exist, that there is good news, light, hope, healing, justice, peace, mercy, joy, and ultimately salvation. That is how God puts us together.

The how of this Gospel is not only the power of its story to shape us, it is to shape us in a particular direction. Matthew moves from light to darkness, from gracious welcome to people left behind or left out. I use the rather awkward term "directionality" to indicate the way the Gospel tells its story. Awkward as the term may be, unless we pay close attention to Matthew's movement, we become like that one-talent individual who presumed that the boss was out to get him (Matt 25). Or, as we might say, he imagined that he had been set up to fail as if life is somehow divinely rigged to punish humanity.

Though Matthew's Gospel has a number of hard sayings, we cannot reverse the direction of God's grace and compassion to project back from the demons of our minds or the valleys of our experience a view of deity that defaces the story. That would be to obscure the good news. However we interpret the hard sayings, and I have generally read them to accent life-and-death matters, we must not make the God of Matthew the opposite of the Savior who has said, "Come unto me all you that are weary and are heavy laden."

Rounding out how the Gospel means, we need to receive it with our whole person, not like someone bobbing for apples at the county fair where only the head goes under. There is always that desire to make something that is coherent into something that is airtight.

I have been saying that God breathes through Matthew and speaks to us from the sacred past to today. Yet, by demanding a kind of logic that lusts to fit everything on the page too snugly with everything else, we put round pegs into square holes, as if Jesus could not address now one situation and later another. In so doing, we suffocate the story, Jesus, and ultimately ourselves in attempting to make God in the image of what we want God to be, mostly a god too small.

Instead, Jesus embraces and upholds our relatedness to God with the magisterial truth of loving God with our whole being, and loving our neighbors as ourselves (Matt 22). As relationships are always in motion, the first and second great commandments on Jesus' lips characterize such love as a journey into the heart of God and with God to the future. In the person of Jesus, love is a journey about the ultimate self-giving of God, the kind we see in its uniqueness on the cross. Or, as Matthew said about him, "He has borne our infirmities and carried our diseases" (8:17; Isa 53:4).

Not only that, I am convinced that everything in Isaiah 53 is referenced by Matthew. "He was wounded for our transgressions, crushed for our iniquities; upon him was the punishment that made us whole, and by his bruises we are healed" (Isa 53:5). What they and we could not do for ourselves, God in the person of Jesus Christ has done that we might become truly whole human beings.

The question *"How does a Gospel mean?"* gets at how Matthew should be read in a way that fits hand-in-glove with its message, which is one of good news and hope. The other question is not unrelated to how Matthew tells the story, but it deepens it: In what ways does Jesus in Matthew show that God is with us, and why does it matter?

In too many words to repeat here, I have made the case that God with Us is Matthew's theme. The author wants us to see in the hero of the story the very presence of God on Earth. But what did that mean and what does it continue to mean?

Jesus said, "I did not come to be served, but to serve" (Matt 20:28). In the great invitation, "Come unto me" (Matt 11:28–30), Jesus said, "I am gentle and humble in heart" (NRSV), but I prefer the older, KJV translation: "I am meek and lowly in heart." God with Us is among the lowly and is like them in their "mean estate." It comes then as no surprise to the reader that the Matthew 25 parable of the nations pictures the judge of all the earth among the least of earth. No wonder that the Savior begins the Sermon on the Mount with the words, "Blessed are the poor in spirit" (Matt 5).

I eschew two extremes in following the Savior. One is to imagine that we live the story best by making ourselves grand. That is what the sons of Zebedee wanted, to sit on Jesus' right and left hand in the kingdom (Matt 20:21). But what they wanted was not his to give (Matt 20:23). God with Us is not all powerful in history. Nothing is more true to the gospel than that, yet, we, like James and John's mother, want "all-powerful." We want to exhibit it to the world, and we want to wrap all our insecurities in it. But that is simply not true to the story.

The other extreme is to imagine that Jesus brought an agenda, namely our agenda, whatever it is. To the contrary, we have seen that zealots, Pharisees, and the leaders of the people could not corral the enigmatic Jesus within their expectations that he be this or that. Instead, Matthew shows us God with Us, a divine presence who did not turn action into agenda nor peace into failure to engage. We cannot make Matthew's holy child into our patron saint. We follow from our need for the very presence of God in the way this prophet and savior will lead us to God.

At the same time, God with Us is not a theme that Matthew shouts in our ears. There are whispers of it that run throughout the first Gospel. Again, Matthew quotes Isaiah, "He will not wrangle or cry aloud, nor will anyone hear his voice in the streets. He will not break a bruised reed or quench a smoldering wick until he brings justice to victory, and in his name the Gentiles will hope" (Matt 12:19–21; Isa 42:2–3 in the Septuagint).[1]

Though Jesus in cleansing the temple was like a bull in a china closet, he normally did not carry a bullhorn and said next to nothing at the end. He was among the people, showing the way. "Tell John what you hear and see" (Matt 11:4–6). When John, isolated within his prison cell, wanted to know whether or not Jesus was the one to come, Jesus replied neither yes nor no but painted a word picture the prophet of the Jordan would recognize from the old scriptures, "The blind receive their sight, the lame walk, the lepers are cleansed, the deaf hear, and the dead are raised, and the poor have good news brought to them, and blessed is anyone who takes no offense at me."

God with Us is about what we hear as a word picture, what we see as it was told in the great story. It comes to us, as to John, into whatever cramped space of heart and mind we dwell and gives us the Holy Spirit as air to breathe. It affords us a worldwide window onto God's presence in history, the inbreaking of resurrection light and a day of hope for all nations. No doubt, our hearts sometimes well up with its vision and strength.

Even so, I pray for a little more humility in church talk, for not all are where we may be. Particularly I pray for greater reticence on the part of some who presume to know God's will. In our pomposity, can we not remember that some lay dying, and others are sore distressed? So, whether we imagine we are building the kingdom by increasing our numbers and influence or placarding church policies to town hall, a little more humility, please. God is with us as we follow persistently and even quietly in demonstrating the story. God is with us as we travel with the telling of sacred story, possibly as a whisper or an unspoken touch at twilight.

On the mountain God is with us as he reinterprets the Law of God and puts it within reach of ordinary people to obey. Even the poor in spirit can stand tall before God as they rise to be the people that God made them, not the recipe others have for them. Matthew's affirmative Jewishness is not a Christianized legalism. It is founded in God's gracious favor toward all people, those Jews thought to be second class and the whole world of Gentiles.

Just as compassion and healing take place before they were signed up for membership, the Beatitudes occur before the demands of the law. God with Us puts obedience to the law within reach of all while offering a yoke

---

1. Rahlfs and Hanhart, *Septuaginta*.

that is easy and a burden that is light (Matt 11:30), not shouldering the people with an impossible weight of guilt or responsibility (Matt 23:4). Jesus in Matthew speaks against replacing the substance with the superficial. We are not to tithe dill, mint, and cummin while neglecting the weightier matters of the law, justice, mercy, and faith (Matt 23:23). Religion is neither a matter of what one wears on the sleeve or finding the speck in a neighbor's eye.

In Matthew, God with Us is the consummate practitioner of the psalmist's words: "God remembers how we were made; God remembers that we are dust" (Ps. 103:14).

Finally, in the much-misunderstood passage regarding the future days in Matthew 24, we may hear the promise of the presence of God coming in the midst of despair as when the temple was torn down by the Romans. We may hear the promise of God's presence coming through the chaos of war as women with nursing babies had to flee for their lives.

When the Twin Towers fell, the victims were not to blame. The story does not place the burden of responsibility upon those whose worlds have fallen apart. Rather, the divine presence offers the very heart of God. Though extreme anguish weighs heavy on Jesus' mind and ours, a profound cry tethers us to heaven.

God with Us is not like a pastor who still takes his check but whose compassion has already retired to a beach and a cool drink. I am not generally critical of pastors because they, like any caregiver, feel that wanderlust to escape their burdens. Rather, we are reclaimed and saved by the message that we are earthenware vessels that hold the treasure (2 Corinthians 4:7). We ourselves are not the treasure.

The treasure of our witness speaks to life when unspeakable suffering collapses trust in any dependable world. Even then, we are not abandoned. All of us want answers, but we are given a hand to hold. We want control of our destinies, but the story offers an everlasting love. At the end of the day, love alone has staying power, and that is what nurses hope and in God's hands gives birth to a new heaven and a new earth.

We travel with Matthew in response to an invitation to take a small part in God's grand story. Whether kneeling at Bethlehem in an ecstasy of joy (Matt 2) or giving a cup of cold water to the least (Matt 10:42), we bend that we may rise. The story shapes us by exercising our days in bending and rising that we may truly find ourselves in losing them in the ongoing history of God with Us

APPENDIX

Confessing Christ for Today

A Sermon Preached Online, June 28, 2020, for Hudson Memorial Presbyterian Church of Raleigh.

When Mac asked me back in the winter to preach this June, like everyone else, I had no idea what hour it would be in our nation's life. Not only that, I didn't know what the lectionary texts would be for the Sundays in mid- to late June.

The text from the lectionary that I have chosen is from Matthew chapter 10. It includes portions from this week and last week, and it is not an easy text, as we have heard.

For a one-off sermon, one might wish for a sweeter passage of Scripture. But a preacher of my age can't bob and weave around every difficult text. Particularly since I have purported to know something about Matthew, how could I? I am convinced that God must have a sense of humor.

Today I follow Mac and Debbie's path in listening to Scripture to hear what the Spirit may be saying to us. Sometimes our situation in life may open our hearts to what we haven't heard before. Let's give it a go. But first, a story closer to home.

I

Near our house, the street ends where it meets the footpath at the woods. Joanna and a neighbor were walking there one day and ran across a teenage girl whose chalk work on the asphalt surface was remarkable. The next day after we had mowed our yard, Joanna took me there to see what the artist called her mini-art gallery.

She had drawn a realistic figure with sad eyes releasing large tears. In another space, she had listed the sad and tragic litany of innocent and unarmed persons of color who have been killed by law enforcement. I knew some of the names but not all. Near the bold letters BLM, for Black Lives Matter, our artist had written, "Grab my hand. We are all in this together."

The teenager's house was next to the path, so Joanna and I rang the doorbell. Her mother came to the door, and we expressed our appreciation for the artwork. She said, "Let me get my daughter, so that she can hear for herself." Standing appropriately distant, I said to the artist, named Destiny, "If it weren't for this virus, I would grab your hand, for we are all in this together. Thank you."

II

The fact that Destiny had put her mini-art gallery on a path used by the whole neighborhood meant to me that her message was for all, black and white. Where we live is a wonderful mix of peoples, much more so than where the manse was located in New York. Just a reminder that the issues that currently plague our nation about race cannot be reduced to the geographic label north and south. We are involved in a struggle that encompasses the whole country.

"Grab my hand. We are all in this together," is, as we know, not original with our Knightdale artist. Nothing about this is original, though it has once more surfaced violently in the ocean of our life with the murder of a particular man, George Floyd.

As we turn to our text in Matthew 10, there are three distinct but related segments. Three "C words" may help us grab onto them: confession of Jesus Christ; confusion about the times; and a new conversation about following Jesus.

First, Jesus pulls no punches. "Whoever confesses me before others, I will confess before my father who is in heaven. Whoever denies me before others, I will deny before my father who is in heaven."

Years ago in a wonderful book on our Presbyterian Confessions, the theologian Jack Rogers reminded us that affirmations or confessions of faith were made at a time of trouble for the church and society. In our Book of Confessions, "The Barmen Declaration" was made as protest when the church in Germany was being coopted by Hitler's Nazi Party. The Confession of 1967, with its major theme of Reconciliation, was made at another time when this nation was being torn apart with protests and riots related to racial inequality.

So, it is timely to confess our faith in Jesus Christ. And in modern America, it may be important to remind ourselves that when we confess the name of Jesus, we are not merely saying a name, we are referencing the whole story of Jesus.

Though Jesus sounds on so many lips across our landscape, we must ask, who is he as identified and shaped by the story of God with Us? Just to say Jesus could mean anything, and has.

As I was leaving a grocery store one day a few months back, I saw a carousel of books and one title got me: *How to Lead Like Jesus*. It's popular to drag Jesus into any discussion that we want to sanction with his name. But *How to Lead like Jesus* sparked what may have been an unkind thought: Does this author know how the story ends?

When we confess Jesus, we are confessing the whole story, incredible joy and abject sorrow; people who are harassed and helpless and a welling up of compassion within the Savior. Confessing Jesus, we are voicing healing in our midst and a hard-nosed prophet of justice for the least among us. Above all, in Matthew we are confessing the story of God with Us who abides our history and leads us to hope through the darkest hour. Even death could not keep him down because God would raise him up.

III

Now, however you look at it, Jesus in Matthew chapter 10 talks about a world in trouble. "Think not that I came to bring peace, but a sword." "A son will turn against his father, and a daughter against her mother." Jesus speaks of a society torn with violent conflict.

What situation is reflected here? Why is Jesus in this portion of the Gospel seemingly different from the rest of Matthew? Afterall, Jesus says, "Blessed are the peacemakers." Not only that, but the Sermon on the Mount has it that Jesus' followers are "to turn the other cheek." Famously he says near the end, "Put your sword away. Those who take up the sword will die that way." I am convinced that Jesus did not want to fashion his followers into a militia to oust the Romans. And Jesus did not want to lead such a fight.

Also in Matthew, Jesus lifts up the Ten Commandments on several occasions. From church school on we have known that the commandments include "Honor your father and mother," so what is going on here? Matthew 10 is anything but a prooftext for family values.

The text cries out for us to read it for its emotional tenor. "Think not that I came to bring peace, rather a sword." "A son will turn against his father and a daughter against her mother." I imagine that those words may further tighten the knots in our stomachs put there by a pandemic without end and peaceful protests met with tear gas.

I suggest that Jesus' words in Matthew 10 reflect a time in which following him was caught up in the Jewish War with the Romans. That is what the faith communities that Matthew wrote to had recently endured. It was a terrible conflict, seven years of it. Up and down Palestine, anyone who got in the way was mowed down, those who had joined up for the fight and shopkeepers just trying to make a living. Then Jerusalem itself was sieged, starved, and sacked. Loyalties were torn, to say the least. Refugees fled for their lives, like those who jumped from rooftops in desperation and others who ran in terror, holding nursing babies.

Our situation is different, of course, but it is, nonetheless, serious. There's a dystopian quality to it if you are familiar with that term. It's an eerie, upside-down time. On a beautiful North Carolina day, we feel like we could go anywhere or do anything, but then suddenly, as if bumping into a glass barrier, we recall there's an invisible pandemic. Ironically our protests of racial injustice move us to "grab one another's hands" and to join our hearts at a time when we need to remain distant from one another for our health's sake.

Yet, even our health has become politically controversial. Do we wear masks or not? Do we go out to eat or not? Is this a hoax or not? Do politicians listen to scientists or not?

We used to say that we are so divided in this country that we can't read time off the same clock. Now, we can't agree on the same science. Two different medical examiners in Minneapolis couldn't agree on what the whole nation has now seen on TV. We are being told one thing, and, yet we see another. Is that dystopian or what? Where is George Orwell when we need him?

But you may want to say, now preacher, people need to get back to work, looters have come on the heels of peaceful protesters, the police are not all bad, and we need 'em, and so on. I'll grant all of that, but the nature of confusion is that something is happening though we abide a cloud of dust that obscures our understanding. Something is happening though there's a fog through which we cannot see. We are traveling blind, and we need a hand to hold.

Jesus has been raised. A new creation is on its way. We cannot turn the clock back. With a sudden flash of light in the dark, we realize the time on our digital devices must be set for a new day.

IV

So, we have confession and confusion, but there's a new way of conversation to which Jesus calls us. "Whoever does not take up the cross and follow me is not worthy of me. Those who find their life will lose it, and those who lose their life for my sake will find it . . . Whoever gives even a cup of cold water to one of these little ones in the name of a disciple—truly I tell you, none of these will lose their reward."

The word "conversation," as we know, means speaking together. But there's an older meaning some of us will remember. Conversation is also a way of life, the way we conduct ourselves.

We confess Jesus in a troubling time that we may find ourselves again in the story of God with Us. When it seems we are coming undone, Jesus invites us back into the story. Let us take up our crosses and follow him. Let us do what we know to do, gestures of justice and kindness for the most needy among us.

I must speak personally here. I grew up in East Texas in a segregated society. In the basement of the county courthouse where my mother worked were those signs I saw as a boy, "For Coloreds Only, For Whites Only."

And yet, in church I learned Jesus' parable of the Good Samaritan. Going down from Jerusalem to Jericho was a journey that, for me, overtook the signs that separated us. I pursued that different way of conversation, making the effort to cross lines of difference.

Now in retirement I watch television and read the news like the rest of you. And I am both discouraged by what I see and stung by some comments I hear.

Did I say enough? Did I do enough? After all these years, are we still at the same place we were? Did what I did for more than forty years matter at all?

Also, I can get defensive. I don't think I was as bad as all that. I did my part. In my mind, I begin to rehearse the way in which I was better than some others or stuck my neck out for the cause.

Like a number of you who also sign the "white" box on forms, I have been listening to and reading black voices. I have been trying to learn where I and we as a society went wrong. I have vacillated between guilt and defensiveness, edging close to the slough of despond.

But then I hear Jesus calling us back into the story. Pick up that cross of guilt and defensiveness and follow. What good will it do you to get stuck in self-pity or bitterness?

Actually, we are where we always were, dependent on the grace of Christ to raise our heads from the ground or from our navels. We were never innocent, just saved sinners.

So, let's listen to the words of Jesus in the art of a girl named Destiny. "Grab my hand. We are all in this together." Or in Matthew 11, "Take my yoke upon you, for I am meek and lowly in heart, and you shall find rest" from the nonsense of trying to justify your sins or wallow in them.

I believe that Christ is calling us to follow in a new day and walk in a new way. We need one another more than ever before. Where there is wrong, let's repent of it. Where we are doing good, let's not be discouraged about it.

Above all, where we can see the face of Christ and feel the Spirit's power, let's reach out for a neighbor's hand, let's learn a new perspective, let's shake off any paralyzing regrets and shame.

This time is like revisiting our baptism as we did in our service and text last week. Dying with Christ, we are raised to walk in a new way of life. We are baptized once, but we die and rise every day to follow Christ on the way. As I listened to Mac last week, I thought of Luther's commentary on Romans 6: "All of life is baptismal in character, which is to say, death and resurrection."

For years now I have loved that song in our hymnal, "Out of Deep Unordered Water." This verse in particular: "Standing round the font reminds us of the Hebrews climb ashore. Life is hallowed by the knowledge, God has been this way before."

So, let us confess our faith again to reenter that old story for a new day. God is with Us. Whatever powers threaten to stake us to the ground, let us uproot our crosses and go with God. "Grab my hand," says the Lord. "We are in this together."

Now, I hand this over to you. God bless.

Bibliography

Abbott, Walter M., S.J., ed. *The Documents of Vatican II*. Baltimore: Geoffrey Chapman, 1966.
Alter, Robert. *The Art of Biblical Narrative*. New York: Basic, 1981.
Anno, Mitsumasa. *Anno's Italy*. New York: William Collins, 1980.
Anderson, Bernhard W. *Understanding the Old Testament*, 4th ed. Englewood Cliffs, New Jersey: Prentice-Hall, 1986.
Auden, W.H. "For the Time Being." *Collected Longer Poems*. New York: Vintage, 1975.
Barth, Karl. *Church Dogmatics: The Doctrine of the Word Of God*. Vol. I, Part One. Edinburgh: T. & T. Clark, 1980.
Bass, Diana Butler. *Christianity after Religion*. New York: HarperOne, 2012.
Berger, Peter L. *The Noise of Solemn Assemblies*. Garden City, New York: Doubleday, 1961.
Bonhoeffer, Dietrich. *The Cost of Discipleship*. New York: Macmillan, 1972.
Borg, Marcus J. *Jesus a New Vision*. New York: Harper Collins, 1991.
Borg, Marcus J. and Crossan, John Dominic. *The Last Week*. New York: HarperCollins, 2006.
Bornkamm, Gunther. *Jesus of Nazareth*. New York: Harper & Row, 1960.
Bowler, Kate. *Everything Happens for a Reason: And Other Lies I've Loved*. New York: Random House, 2018.
Brown, Raymond. E. *An Introduction to the New Testament*. New York: Doubleday, 1997.
Brunner, Emil. *The Divine Imperative*. Philadelphia: Westminster, 1937.
Buber, Martin. *On the Bible: Eighteen Studies*. New York: Schocken, 1982.
Bultmann, Rudolph. *Jesus and the Word*. London: Collins Fontana, 1958.
–––. *Existence and Faith*. New York: World Publishing, 1963.
Caird, G.B. *The Language and Imagery of the Bible*. Philadelphia: Westminster, 1980.
Chesterton, G.K. *Orthodoxy*. Garden City, New York: Image, 1959.
–––. *The Complete Father Brown*. Hammondsworth, Middlesex, UK: Penguin, 1986.
Ciardi, John. "How Does a Poem Mean? (1962)" *Augsburg University Archives, Youtube*. August 16, 2018. https://www.youtube.com/watch?v=h_Tam5sHa4k.
Cross, F.L. and E.A. Livingstone, eds.*The Oxford Dictionary of the Christian Church*. Oxford: Oxford University PRess, 1984.
Davies, W.D. and Allison, Dale C., Jr. *A Critical and Exegetical Commentary on the Gospel According to Saint Matthew*. Vol. I (Matthew 1–7), Vol. II (Matthew 8–13),

Vol. III (Matthew 19–28). International Critical Commentary. Edinburgh: T. & T. Clark, 2004.

Dibelius, Martin. *Jesus*. Philadelphia: Westminster, 1949.

Donne, John. *John Donne Devotions*. Ann Arbor: University of Michigan Press, 1975.

Fackenheim, Emil L. *God's Presence in History*. New York: Harper, 1972.

Free Expression. "Peter Ustinov talks, hilariously, about making Spartacus, Charles Laughton, and more." *Blogspot.com* May 14, 2019.

Eliot, T.S. *The Complete Poems and Plays*. New York: Harcourt, Brace & World, 1971.

Hadden, Jeffrey K. *The Gathering Storm in the Churches*. Garden City, New York: Anchor, 1970.

Hays, Richard B. *Reading Backwards*. Waco, Texas: Baylor University Press, 2014.

Herberg, Will. *Protestant-Catholic-Jew*. Garden City, New York: Doubleday, 1956.

Herbert, George. *George Herbert: The Country Parson and the Temple*. New York: Paulist, 1981.

Hoge, Dean R. *Division in the Protestant House*. Philadelphia: Westminster, 1976.

James, William. *The Varieties of Religious Experience*. New York: New American Library, 1958.

Johnson, Barry. *Polarity Management: Identifying and Managing Unsolvable Problems*. Amherst, Massachusetts: HRD Press, 1996.

Johnson, Samuel. *The Selected Writings of Samuel Johnson*. New York: New American Library, 1981.

Kafka, Franz. *Selected Stories of Franz Kafka*. New York: Modern Library, 1952.

Kolbert, Elizabeth. Photos by Robin Hammond. "Skin Deep: What is Race Exactly?" *National Geographic*. Vol. 233, No. 4. (April 2018) 29–41.

Kierkegaard, Soren. *Parables of Kierkegaard*. Ed. Thomas C. Oden. Princeton, New Jersey: Princeton University Press, 1989.

Metzger, Bruce M., *Lexical Aids for Students of New Testament Greek*. Princeton, New Jersey: Published by the Author, New Edition, 1980.

Metzger, Bruce M., and Roland E. Murphy, eds. *The New Oxford Annotated Bible: New Revised Standard Version*. New York: Oxford University Press, 1991.

O'Connor, Flannery. *Mystery and Manners*. New York: Farrar, Straus & Giroux, 1969.

Pascal, Blaise. *Pascal's Pensees*. New York: Dutton, 1958.

Rahlfs, Alfred, and Robert Hanhart, eds. *Septuaginta*. Stuttgart: Deutsche Bibelgesellschaft, 1935.

Schurer, Emil. *The Jewish People in the Time of Jesus Christ*. Edinburgh: T. & T. Clark, 1890.

Shinn, Roger L. *Tangled World*. New York: Charles L. Scribner's Sons, 1965.

Sittler, Joseph A. *Joseph A. Sittler: Grace Notes and Other Fragments*. Philadelphia: Fortress, 1982.

Stendahl, Krister. "The Apostle Paul and the Introspective Conscience of the West." *Harvard Theological Review*. Vol. 56, Issue 3. (July 1963) 199–215.

Taylor, Charles. *Sources of the Self: The Making of the Modern Identity*. Cambridge, Massachusetts: Harvard University Press, 1989.

Terkel, Studs. *Working: People Talk About What They Do All Day and How They Feel About What They Do*. New York City: New Press, 1997.

The Book of Confessions, "The Confession of 1967." Louisville, Kentucky: The Office of the General Assembly, 1994.

Theissen, Gerd. *Sociology of Early Palestinian Christianity*. Philadelphia: Fortress, 1982.

Twells, Henry. "At Even, When the Sun Was Set." Hymn 343. *Great Songs of the Church*. No. 2. Chicago: Great Songs, 1969.
Wiesel, Elie. *Five Biblical Portraits*. Notre Dame: University of Notre Dame Press, 1981.
Winter, Gibson. *The Suburban Captivity of the Churches*. New York: Macmillan, 1962.
Wittgenstein, Ludwig. *Philosophical Investigations*. New York: Macmillan, 1968.
Wright, N.T. *The New Testament and the People of God*. Minneapolis: Fortress, 1992.
Yeats, William Butler. *Selected Poems and Two Plays of William Butler Yeats*. New York: Collier, 1976.

www.ingramcontent.com/pod-product-compliance
Lightning Source LLC
Chambersburg PA
CBHW070922180426
43192CB00037B/1709